LAF

Grammar Matters

Mark Smee

with contributions from John Dayus

Heinemann

Heinemann Educational Publishers
Halley Court, Jordan Hill, Oxford OX2 8EJ
Part of Harcourt Education

Heinemann is the registered trademark of
Harcourt Education Limited

First published 1997

06

15 14

10-digit ISBN: 0 435224 68 9
13-digit ISBN: 978 0 435224 68 9

Designed and typeset by Ken Vail Graphic Design
Illustrated by Judy Brown and Maggie Ling
Cover design by MCC
Printed and bound in Edinburgh by Scotprint

Acknowledgements

The Authors and Publishers would like to thank the following for permission to
use photographs/copyright material:

Extracts on p12 (adapted), p74, p77 (adapted introduction) from 'Flowers for the new girl' by Vivien Alcock ©
Vivien Alcock from *No More School* ed Valerie Bierman, Methuen Children's Books: Jennifer Johnson (Authors'
Agent) Ltd; extract A on p19 adapted from *Red Sky in the Morning* by Elizabeth Laird © Elizabeth Laird:
reprinted by permission of Heinemann Young Books (a division of Reed Int. Books Ltd); extract B on p19
(adapted) and p83 from *Boy* by Roald Dahl © Roald Dahl, Jonathan Cape: David Higham Associates; extract on
p23 adapted from *The Lost Boy* by George Mackay Brown © George Mackay Brown: John Murray (Publishers)
Ltd; extracts on p31,74 from *Whispers in the Graveyard* by Theresa Breslin © Theresa Breslin: Methuen
Children's Books; extracts on pp39, 40, 41 from *Wicked* by Anthony Masters © Anthony Masters: Orchard
Publishers: extract on p45 from *The Play of Goggle Eyes* by Anne Fine (Heinemann, 1995, adapted from the
1989 Hamish Hamilton novel) Novel copyright © Anne Fine, 1989, play copyright © Anne Fine, 1995.
Reprinted by permission of Penguin Books Ltd; extract on p57 adapted from 'When Schooldays turn into
Nightmares', published in *Living Magazine* 1990; advertisement on p69 'Bearbaiting', Libearty Campaign:
WSPA; extract on p79 from the autobiographical introduction to 'What's for Dinner?' by Robert Swindells from
No More School ed Valerie Bierman, Methuen Children's Books: Jennifer Luithlen Agency; extract on p81
adapted from 'Car clamper rises to new heights' by Randeep Rameesh, *The Independent* 3/1/92: The
Independent; extract on p91 from *The Wreck of the Zanzibar* by Michael Morpurgo © Michael Morpurgo:
William Heinemann Ltd.

The Publishers have made every effort to trace the copyright holders, but if they have
inadvertently overlooked any, they will be pleased to make the necessary arrangements at the
first opportunity.

The Publishers would like to thank the World Society for the Protection of Animals for permission to
reproduce the photo on page 69.

Grammar Matters is designed to make learning about grammar enjoyable and accessible to Key Stage 3 students. It is clearly structured so that students gain a coherent picture of how language works.

Throughout the book, the emphasis is firmly on students' own writing. Students are encouraged to use the knowledge and understanding they gain to help them reflect on their writing. Lively writing activities encourage students to develop their skills. Reading response activities help students to focus closely on how language is used and to develop their critical awareness. The emphasis on learning grammar within meaningful reading and writing activities is very much in line with the development of Key Stage 3 assessment.

We offer progression throughout the book by beginning with terms and concepts which are familiar to many Key Stage 3 students and moving on to explore sentence grammar and whole texts. The sentence work in Units 3 and 4 is not more difficult than the work on word classes in Unit 2. However, as our research shows that sentence grammar has not been widely taught in schools recently we felt it would be helpful to teachers and students to begin with more familiar work on words and word classes. The book is organised in clear, double-page spreads so you can use individual spreads for particular needs or work through the book. Revision sections help students to consolidate their learning. The final sections, Units 6 and 7 are intended to be dipped into to meet individual needs.

This book is accompanied by a photocopiable Teacher's Resource Pack which offers homework sheets, extra support for lower-ability students and answers to the Student Book activities.

Contents

Contents

Unit 1: Words

In this unit we look at how words are made up of different parts. Understanding how words are formed will:

- help you to *spell* words
- help you to understand how words are built up.

One word can often be used to make others by adding letter strings.

Take the word *play*:

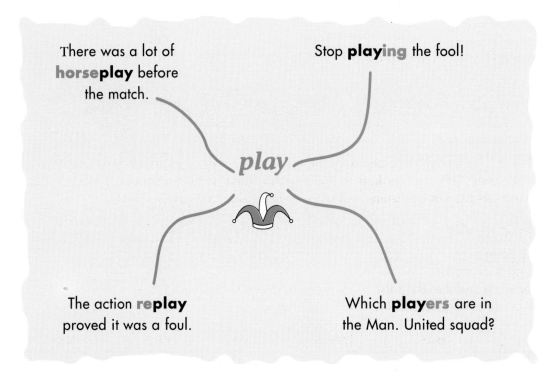

There was a lot of **horseplay** before the match.

Stop **playing** the fool!

play

The action **replay** proved it was a foul.

Which **players** are in the Man. United squad?

Activity 1

With a partner, see how many more words you can make from the word **play**.

Prefixes and suffixes

If a letter string is added in front of a word, it is called a **prefix**. If it is added after a word, it is called a **suffix**.

Disallow		**Unhelpful**			**Jumping**	
Prefix	Word	Prefix	Word	Suffix	Word	Suffix

Prefixes and Suffixes

Activity 2

1 Write out the following words and underline the **prefixes**:

disobey   supermarket   defrost   uncaring   inability

Can you guess what these prefixes mean? What difference does it make if you cross them out?

2 Write out the following words and underline the **suffixes**:

sadness   laughable   playing   helpful   enjoyment

Activity 3

Here are some examples of common prefixes:

un-	**under-**	**over-**	**re-**	**pre-**
uncooked	undercooked	overcooked	recooked	precooked
unpaid	underpaid	overpaid	repaid	prepaid

1 Make a table like the one below. In the first column write a sentence using each of the above forms of **cooked**. In the second column write a second sentence which has the same meaning, but *without* using the prefix. For example:

With prefix	**Without prefix**
My egg was uncooked.	My egg was not cooked.

2 With a partner, make a list of words which will begin with at least two of the prefixes. Use a table like the one below.

	un-	**under-**	**over-**	**re-**	**pre-**
dress	undress	underdress	overdress		
do	undo		overdo	redo	

Activity 4

Some of the most important **suffixes** in English are: -ing   -ed   -d

Use a table like the one below to write down five more words that can end with **-ing** and either **-ed** or **-d**.

Note: for some words there is a slight change in spelling: *love/loving*. Use a dictionary to help you.

Word	Ending		
	-ing	**-ed**	**-d**
wash	washing	washed	
shop	shopping	shopped	
love	loving		loved

Prefixes, Suffixes and Stems

Activity 5

1 Below is a list of words and a list of common suffixes. Work out which of the suffixes can be added to each word and write down all the possibilities. Some words will need spelling changes, so use your dictionary to help you.

joy	slow	wonder		-ment	-ful	-ly
happy	amaze	sing		-ness	-ing	-fully

2 Write a sentence for each word you have made to show how it is used.

Stems

The **stem** is the main part of the word:

prefix   stem   suffix

un + fair + ness

The stem is often a word in its own right (like **fair**) but it may not be. For example: expel, impel and repel have the same stem **-pel**, but this is not a word on its own.

Activity 6

1 With a partner, choose **one** of the following words:

shop   wash
print   work   dog

Make a list of all the words that you can create by adding prefixes and suffixes. Use the examples in this unit to help you.

2 Now add prefixes and suffixes to your words to make up new words you have never seen before. Write all your new words in a column. Next to each one, write:
● what you think it could mean
● a sentence which includes the word.

Example:

workful – *hard-working* – 'Gemma is very **workful**.'

Prefixes, Suffixes and Stems extension

Activity 7

In the sentences below, a number of stems appear in brackets. For the sentences to make sense, these stems need to have either prefixes or suffixes added to them. A few will need both. Work out what the complete words should be, using the sense of each sentence to help you. Write out the complete sentences.

1 I (**decide**) that it was time to stop (**believe**) everything she told me.

2 (**Fortunate**), Gary (**slip**) on the muddy top step, fell (**heavy**) to the ground and broke his arm.

3 It was very (**kind**) of you to shout at Wendy like that especially when she (**help**) you so much yesterday.

4 What a sight! She was (**wear**) the most (**outrage**) orange trousers you've ever seen, with a (**repulse**) pea-green top and (**sick**) pink eyeliner.

5 (**Prolong**) exposure to the sun without (**protect**) can result in (**harm**) sunburn, with the risk of (**contract**) skin cancer.

6 They don't like (**have**) to fill in forms instead of being (**interview**), because they feel it's so (**person**).

Summary

Stem This is the main part of a word. It can be a word in its own right (like **fair**) but it may not be.

Prefix This comes before the stem. It changes the meaning of the stem in some way.

Suffix This comes after the stem. It changes the way the stem can be used.

Unit 2: Words and phrases

> Words can be put into **classes** according to the job they do in a sentence. In this unit you will learn how words work in sentences and how to identify words according to the job they are doing. The grammatical terms you learn will help you to discuss your own writing.

Nouns

Nouns are words for people, places, things, activities and states.

1   The **vicar** takes the **service** at our **church**.

2   Our **dog** likes to chew **Dad's newspaper**.

3   I play **tennis** with **Nasreen** on **Tuesdays**.

4   **Drunkenness** is dangerous.

5   You don't care about my **feelings**.

People	Places	Things	Activities	States
vicar Dad Nasreen	church	service dog newspaper feelings Tuesdays	tennis	drunkenness

Activity 1

For each sentence opposite think of three nouns that will complete it. In your sentences include at least one **person**, one **thing**, one **activity** and one **state**.

- This is a _____ .
- _____ is a good thing.
- Have you got any _____?
- I like _____ .

Nouns

Activity 2

Write down a noun for every blank label on the picture. Your choices
must include at least one of the following:

> a noun for a **person**
>
> a noun for a **thing**
>
> a noun for an **activity**
>
> a noun for a **state.**

For example, if you think the couple on the wall are showing **happiness**,
that could be your **state** noun.

Activity 3

Now write a description of what is happening in the picture. Include the
nouns you listed for Activity 2.

Nouns

Activity 4

1 Which of the **bold** words below are nouns? Write them down.

> **Barbara** lost a pound **coin** out of the **pocket** of her cardigan, which she had **hung** over the back of her chair in the **canteen**. She said somebody must have stolen it while she and her friends were **queuing** for their sausage and **chips**. She looked straight at **Jo when** she **said** this, so of course we all looked at Jo, too.

2 How did you work out which words are nouns? Discuss your method with a partner.

3 Now look at the next part of the story, which has some gaps where nouns should be. Choose suitable nouns to fill these gaps.

> 'It wasn't me,' she said, but she flushed scarlet and her _____ filled with _____. Everybody thought she was guilty.
>
> 'Give it back to me,' _____ said, holding out her _____. 'Give it back right now, or you'll be sorry. You'll wish you'd never been born.'
>
> 'I haven't got it!' _____ cried, and now her _____ spilled over. 'I never touched your _____!'
>
> 'Let's search her,' somebody said.
>
> We all moved towards her and she fled, out of the _____ and down the _____, running like a terrified _____ looking for a dark _____ to hide in.

4 Continue the story in your own words. When you have finished, underline ten nouns in your writing.

Extension

Give your partner a copy of your story with ten nouns blanked out. Ask your partner to think of nouns to fill the ten gaps.

Nouns

Plurals

To make most nouns plural add **s**: cup cup**s**	To make nouns that end in **s**, **x**, **ch**, **sh** plural add **es**: church church**es**

To make nouns that end in **y** plural:

add **s** if the letter before the **y** is *a, e, o* or *u*:   boy   boy**s**

remove the **y** and add **ies** if the letter before the **y** is a consonant: lady   lad**ies**

To make nouns that end in **f** or **fe** plural change **f/fe** to **ves**: leaf lea**ves** life li**ves** **Exceptions:** all words that end in **ff** take **s**: cliff cliffs. **So do:** dwarf, roof, reef, fife, belief, grief, waif.	There are no rules for making words that end in **o** into plurals. You will need to use your dictionary if you are unsure. Most take **s** or **es**: piano piano**s** potato potato**es**

Note: Remember **not** to put an apostrophe in plural nouns.

Activity 5

Write down the plural forms of the nouns in brackets:

> *Danny woke slowly from a happy dream. He had just scored three (try) and two (penalty) and was feeling like the best of his (hero). There was a curious shape at the bottom of his bed and, for a moment, he thought (thief) had visited during the night. Then, kicking himself for being so stupid, he pounced on his Christmas stocking. Inside he found two (box) of (chocolate), three (orange) and two football (video). He was dying to wake his mother to give her his present of six new crystal (glass) and some new kitchen (knife). However, he had promised to let her sleep until 7.30. He lay back and tried to think of an answer to the question his six-year-old brother had asked the night before: How does Santa Claus visit (family) living in houses without (chimney)?*

Summary
Nouns are words for people, places, things, activities and states.

Pronouns

Nouns are vital to language because we need to be able to name things. However, we can have too many of them:

> *John went to the canteen. John ordered fried eggs, chips and baked beans. John added a large glass of Coke and a bowl of chocolate pudding to John's tray, before paying and making John's way to John's seat. But John didn't make it: John tripped on the strap of John's bag and emptied the whole trayful into a man's lap. It was the headteacher's...*

Activity 1

Re-write the paragraph above. Leave the first word, but replace most of the other *Johns* with other words to make the paragraph flow more easily.

Pronouns

1 You have probably replaced most of the *Johns* above with **he**. **He** is a **personal pronoun**.

Personal pronouns stand for people or things:							
Singular:	**I**	**me**	**you**	**he**	**she**	**him**	**her**	**it**
Plural:	**We**	**us**	**you**	**they**	**them**			

2 You may have replaced *John's seat* with **his** seat. **His** is a **possessive pronoun**.

Possessive pronouns stand for people or things that have or own something:							
Singular:	**my**	**mine**	**your**	**yours**	**her**	**hers**	**his**	**its**
Plural:	**our**	**ours**	**your**	**yours**	**their**	**theirs**		

Pronouns

Activity 2

Use a chart like this to make a list of the personal pronouns and possessive pronouns which appear in the story below. Decide whether the pronouns are singular or plural.

	Personal pronoun	Possessive pronoun
Singular	he	his
Plural		

John couldn't believe his bad luck. He stood rooted to the spot, paralysed with embarrassment and unable to utter even one word of apology. The headteacher was sitting in the dining hall because he was showing some very important visitors around the school. The headteacher leapt to his feet and, as he did so, he knocked a glass of water over one of the visitors. The visitor, a prim lady in her early fifties, stood up. She began to dry herself with a handkerchief. A few people round the hall began to laugh but their laughter soon died when they saw how red and angry the headteacher looked. He began to apologise to the visitor:

'I'm so sorry,' he offered her his handkerchief, 'Here, take mine. It's larger.'

Then, as if suddenly remembering how the incident started, the headteacher turned to face John who was standing still, looking stunned. Everyone was staring at them.

'You, boy! How did you manage to do something so stupid? Get a cloth and clear this mess up.'

'I'm really sorry,' John mumbled to him.

Stirred into action, an auxiliary rushed to the kitchen to get a cloth. The headteacher turned to sit back down in his seat and tripped over John's bag which was still lying where John had dropped it. As he sprawled wildly down the hall, the headteacher yelled:

'Whose is that? What is it doing in the middle of the floor?'

Pronouns

First person or third person?

The story about John is told in the third person – as a 'he' story. Another way to tell the story is to tell it as an 'I' story – in the first person. Telling stories as 'I' stories helps us to get inside characters' heads so we know exactly what they are thinking and feeling.

Activity 3

Rewrite the story about John as an 'I' story. You may add extra descriptions of how John is feeling and explain what he thinks about the headteacher.

Caution: even when possessive pronouns end with the letter **s** you never use an apostrophe with them.

Don't use too many!

Read this version of the story about John. What makes it difficult to work out what is going on?

> *Then, as if suddenly remembering how the incident started, he turned to face him. He was standing still, looking stunned. Everyone was staring at them.*
>
> *'You, boy! How did you manage to do something so stupid? Get a cloth and clear this mess up.'*
>
> *'I'm really sorry,' he mumbled.*
>
> *Stirred into action, an auxiliary rushed to the kitchen to get a cloth. He turned to sit back down in his seat and tripped over his bag which was still lying where he had dropped it. As he sprawled wildly down the hall, he yelled:*
>
> *'Whose is that? What is it doing in the middle of the floor?'*

Using too many pronouns is a common fault in students' writing. If you don't use enough nouns and proper names the reader can't work out what is happening or who is speaking!

Activity 4

Continue the story of John. Try to use pronouns to help your writing flow more clearly. Remember not to use too many pronouns and to make sure the reader can always understand who is speaking.

Pronouns extension

There are several other kinds of pronouns:

1 **Reflexive pronouns** refer back to a noun or personal pronoun:

Singular: **myself**   **yourself**   **herself**   **himself**   **itself**

Plural: **ourselves**   **yourselves**   **themselves**

Example: ***Students*** *should test* ***themselves***.

Themselves is a reflexive pronoun because the students *themselves* are testing *themselves*.

In the sentence 'Students should test this **themselves**', **themselves** is *not* a reflexive pronoun because the students are testing something else. This use is sometimes called an emphatic pronoun.

Further examples: *You must prepare* ***yourself****! She saw* ***herself*** *in the mirror. He defended* ***himself****.*

2 **Relative pronouns** appear in the second part of a sentence when we want to refer back to a noun in the first part:

who   **whose**   **whom**   **which**

Examples: *Penny is a confident* ***girl who*** *likes to be independent.*
             We live in ***Dunchester, which*** *is fifteen miles from the school.*

3 **Interrogative pronouns** are used for asking questions:

who?   **which?**   **whom?**   **whose?**   **what?**

Examples: ***What*** *are you doing?*
             Who *was that boy I saw you with last night?*

4 **Demonstrative pronouns** stand for things we want to point out:

this   **that**   **these**   **those**

Examples: *Do you want* ***this****?*
             I'd like seven of ***these*** *and four of* ***those****, please.*

Activity 5

Look back at the story of John on page 15. Find an example of:
● a demonstrative pronoun   ● a reflexive pronoun
● an interrogative pronoun   ● a relative pronoun.

Activity 6

Look at a piece of your recent writing. Underline the pronouns and decide what type each pronoun is.

Summary

Pronouns are words such as **I**, **she**, **mine**, **it**, **which**, **those**. We use pronouns in place of nouns in sentences to help our writing flow more clearly.

Adjectives

Activity 1

1 Make a list of words to fill the spaces below.

> Leaning back in a wicker chair sat Doctor Pimm, a plump, red-faced man with a shiny, _____ head and _____, beady eyes. His wife, Jane, a tall, _____, freckled woman with closely cropped iron-grey hair, sat opposite him. Doctor Pimm usually avoided introducing his wife to people as she was rude and vicious.

2 Write down words to fill the spaces in the advertisement below.

> **Twill Cottage**
> A _____ , traditional cottage in the _____ village of Quainton. A _____ stream runs through the garden. There are two _____ bedrooms upstairs and a kitchen and large living room downstairs. Ideal location within walking distance of the village centre.

Adjectives

The words which fit the spaces above are **adjectives**. Adjectives are sometimes known as describing words because we use them to say more about nouns.

Adjectives may be placed before the noun:

> ...a **tall**, **thin**, **freckled** woman...

or after verbs like *be*, *seem*, *appear*, *become*:

> ...she was **rude** and **vicious**.

When a number of adjectives are used together to describe a noun they appear in a particular order:

> A **gorgeous**, **long**, **black** dress...

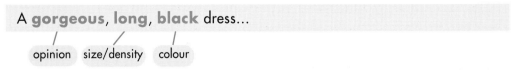

opinion   size/density   colour

Adjectives

Activity 2

1 Here are two descriptions with blanks where the adjectives should be. Choose adjectives from the box below to fill in the blanks. Make sure that each passage as a whole makes sense and write out your finished version.

a *She was one of the most _____ people I've ever seen. She's got this _____ _____ _____ hair, that she can flick about her face and it falls back into place, like on the shampoo ads. And she's got a _____, _____ nose, and perfectly _____teeth, and _____ skin covered with a sort of bloom, like a peach, and _____ _____ eyes that are _____ and _____ like a spaniel's.*

b *She was a _____ _____ _____ hag with a moustache on her upper lip and a mouth as _____ as a _____ gooseberry. Her apron was _____ and _____. Her blouse had bits of breakfast all over it, toast crumbs and tea stains and splotches of dried egg-yolk. It was her hands, however, that disturbed us most. They were _____. They were _____ with dirt and grime.*

long	small	even	grey
skinny	luscious	old	beautiful
transparent	sour	wonderful	greasy
huge	green	disgusting	deep
big	fine	brown	chestnut
black			

2 How did you decide where to place the adjectives? What clues did the texts give you?

Activity 3

1 Turn the positive image of the woman in the first description into a negative image by using different adjectives. You may use adjectives of your own choosing.

2 Swap your description with your partner and comment on each other's choice of adjectives. Who has created the most negative description?

Adjectives

> When we compare one thing with another, we use a **comparative** adjective:

Mandy is **shorter** than her sister.

Mandy   Rachel

Rachel is the **taller**.

> When comparing more than two things, we use a **superlative** adjective:

Mandy is the **shortest**

Mandy   Tom   Rachel

Rachel is the **tallest**

1 If an adjective only has **one syllable** (vowel sound), we make the comparative form by adding -**er**, and the superlative form by adding -**est**, to the adjective:

	Comparative	Superlative
high	high**er**	high**est**
light	light**er**	light**est**
big	bigg**er**	bigg**est**

Notice that **big** needs a double **g** in comparative and superlative form.

2 If an adjective has **more than two** syllables, we make the comparative by putting **more** in front of the adjective and the superlative by putting **most** in front of the adjective:

	Comparative	Superlative
interesting	**more** interesting	**most** interesting
reliable	**more** reliable	**most** reliable

Adjectives

3   Adjectives with **exactly two** syllables can be formed in either way. For these, your best guide is what sounds natural to you.

Some only sound right with the suffixes:

	Comparative	Superlative
narrow	narrow**er**	narrow**est**
silly	silli**er**	silli**est**

Some only sound right with **more** and **most**:

	Comparative	Superlative
afraid	**more** afraid	**most** afraid
awful	**more** awful	**most** awful

4   Finally, there are a few adjectives which change completely for the comparative and superlative forms. Here are the most common ones:

	Comparative	Superlative
good	better	best
bad	worse	worst
many	more	most
little	less	least

Activity 4

Replace the adjective in brackets with the right **comparative** form:

1   Her writing is (**neat**) than his.
2   Please be (**careful**) with that axe, Linda.
3   I feel much (**happy**) since my brother took up bungee jumping.
4   He couldn't have been (**horrible**) towards poor old Edwin.
5   Our DJ feels that the Nice Girls will have a (**big**) hit than last time.

Activity 5

Replace the adjective in brackets with the right **superlative** form:

1   *First Among Equals* is the (**boring**) book I've ever read.
2   The new Lada Hedgehog GTi is the (**quick**) and (**flashy**) car on the block.
3   When Sir mixed the powders together, there was the (**almighty**) bang.
4   By pouring cement into my handbag, you went just the (**tiny**) bit too far.
5   Darryl's the (**gorgeous**) hunk I've ever met.

Adjectives: Your own writing

Read the advertisements below.

Hotel Colon

 Active young people looking for a good time will love the Hotel Colon.

The hotel is right in the middle of the bustling town centre, only a short walk from the beach. In the town centre you will find plenty of restaurants, late-night bars and the wildest discos around! The hotel has:

● *massive swimming pool with sun terrace and bar*
● *fifties bar with pool table*
● *spacious games and video room.*

Hotel Maria

 For those who want a restful holiday, a small friendly hotel.

The Hotel Maria is situated in a pleasant area away from the busy town centre. It is very close to a secluded beach. It offers service at a reasonable price and has:

● *a small, sunny swimming pool*
● *an air-conditioned dining room with piano music*
● *a quieter, comfortable lounge with bar and food.*

Activity 1

1 Identify the adjectives in each advert. Write down the adjectives and nouns they are describing in a chart like the one opposite. If you find a comparative or superlative adjective, then note it on your chart.

Hotel Colon	Hotel Maria
active young people	**small friendly** hotel

2 How do the adjectives help to build a picture of each hotel and its surroundings?

Activity 2

Write your own advertisement for the hotel below. Use the format of the advertisements above. Use adjectives to make your meaning clearer.

Your hotel: a hotel suitable for a family holiday. There is something to keep everyone happy – something for children, teenagers and adults.

Adjectives extension

Activity 1

Read the passage below:

> The road through the village was deep in snow, dark except where under old Scabra's window the lamplight had stained it an orange colour. The snow shadows were blue under his walls. The stars were like sharp nails. Even though I had wrapped my scarf twice around my neck, I shivered in the bitter night.
>
> Where could I go? The warm light in the old villain's window was entrancing – I fluttered towards it like a moth. How would such a sour old creature be celebrating Christmas Eve? Thinking black thoughts beside his fire, stroking his wicked one-eyed cat.
>
> The snow crashed like thin fragile glass under my feet.
>
> I stood at last outside the fisherman's window. I looked in.
>
> There was no crotchety old man inside, no one-eyed cat, no ingrained filth and hung cobwebs. A boy I had never seen before was sitting at the table. He might have been about my own age and his head was a mass of bronze ringlets.

Look at the adjectives 'sharp' and 'bitter' in paragraph 1 and 'warm' and 'entrancing' in paragraph 2. Why do you think the author has chosen each word? What contrast do these adjectives create between the inside and the outside?

Activity 2

Choose three other adjectives from the passage above. Explain why you think the author chose each adjective and how each adjective helps to paint a vivid picture for the reader.

Summary
- **Adjectives** are sometimes known as 'describing words' because we use them to say more about nouns.
- **Comparative adjectives** compare one thing with another.
- **Superlative adjectives** compare more than two things.

Verbs

Activity 1

Think of words to fit the spaces in the paragraph below:

> We _____ slowly along the street, enjoying the lazy
> afternoon sunshine. For a joke I suddenly _____ my
> ball at Jo. To our horror it _____ straight through the
> newsagent's window.

How many different words can you think of for each blank? Compare
your choices with a partner's.

Verbs

The words which fit into the spaces above are **verbs**. Verbs are
incredibly important – it is difficult to write a sentence which makes
sense without one. You may have heard verbs described as 'doing' words
or words which describe actions. However, they not only tell us about
what someone or something is *doing*. They also describe *feelings* and
thoughts. Some of the most important verbs are *being* and *having*
words, from the verbs 'to be' and 'to have'.

Denzil **plays** football for the school team.

plays expresses what Denzil does.

I **worry** a lot about homework.

worry expresses how 'I' feel.

It **was** late when we got home.

was is a 'being' word, which tells
us the state of something – in this
case, the time.

He **imagines** that I admire him.

imagines expresses how 'he' thinks.

We **had** a great meal at McDrongos.

had is a 'having' word.

Activity 2

Choose suitable **verbs** to go in the spaces provided:

1 I _____ that he's a kind person, but Sharon doesn't like him.

2 Terry says he _____ no idea where he put it.

3 They _____ only sixteen when they first met.

4 I _____ the bike carefully.

5 He's not that keen on tennis but he _____ Wimbledon.

Verbs

Activity 3

With your partner think of verbs to fit the spaces in the passage below.
Try to make:

- one version in which Mr Beech is the sweetest teacher in the world and 9W the most rowdy class
- one version in which Mr Beech is a tyrant and 9W a very well-behaved class.

Here are some words you might use:

shouted	wandered	asked	smiling	hurried	smiled
stormed	bellowed	yelling	shuffled	glared	told
chattering	whispering	got	grumbling	glanced	gestured

Mr Beech _____ into the classroom after break and _____ at 9W to be quiet. 9W stopped _____ at each other and _____ into their seats. Mr Beech _____ at them and told them to get their books out of their bags quickly. The students unpacked their books, _____ to each other as they did so. Mr Beech _____ at them again.

Activity 4

Write a short paragraph about your journey to school this morning. Were you in a hurry? Was your journey fast or slow? Who did you meet as you came into school? What were they doing?

Try to use interesting verbs to describe your actions.

25

Verbs — how many words?

The verb in a sentence may be one word or more than one word. The verbs in this paragraph are in **bold**:

> I **played** my new song to my friends last night. I **had been practising** the song for weeks and they **couldn't believe** how brilliant it **was**! I usually **play** my guitar and **sing** every night when I **get** home from school. I **am going to form** a group when I **leave** school. I **might be** famous one day.

When we are talking about verbs in sentences we call the verb the **verb phrase**. The verb phrase may be one word or more than one word.

Activity 1

Working with a partner, make a list of the **verb phrases** in the following sentences. Try to make sure you get *all* the words that form the verb phrase.

Remember: verbs are *doing*, *thinking*, *feeling*, *having* and *being* words.

1 Everyone was fascinated by my story.
2 Danny was chilled right through by the time he arrived home.
3 I am sick of the mess you always leave in the kitchen.
4 'He has such a winning smile,' she said.
5 After Debbie had walked around outside for a few minutes, she felt better.
6 He thought that he recognised the face, but he wasn't sure.
7 I understand that you chased Billy around the classroom with a water pistol.
8 I might play football tonight.

Verb phrases

Auxiliary verbs

Look at the verb phrases you listed in Activity 1. Each verb phrase contains a **main** verb.

In the sentence:

> I might **play** football tonight.   **play** is a main verb.

The other verbs in the sentence are known as **auxiliary verbs**.

> I **might** play football tonight.   **might** is an auxiliary verb.

Auxiliary verbs help the main verb to express its meaning.

Some verb phrases contain more than one auxiliary verb:

> She **had been** **writing** music for years.
>
> auxiliary verb   auxiliary verb   main verb

Here are some more examples of auxiliary verbs:

> He **is** tidying his bedroom.
> He **will** tidy his bedroom.
> He **may** tidy his bedroom.
> He **should** tidy his bedroom.
> He **must** tidy his bedroom.
> He **could be** tidying his bedroom.

Some auxiliary verbs are often abbreviated:

*I **am** going* becomes ***I'm** going*. The auxiliary verb is just the ***m***.

Activity 2

Look again at the list of verb phrases you made for Activity 1. Divide each verb phrase which has more than one word into auxiliary and main verbs. Use a table like the one below.

auxiliary	main

Verb phrases

Activity 3

Write out the following paragraph, putting **auxiliary verbs** in the spaces provided:

> Ray walked slowly over to the bike. He suddenly felt
> a temptation to sit on it. He glanced quickly at the bar. He
> _____ see the bike's owner waiting to be served.
> Ray swung his leg over the seat and sat astride the
> machine. He _____ dying to ride the bike. Ray
> knew that if he took the bike the owner _____ come
> out of the pub before he returned. However, he
> _____ see that the owner still _____ not
> been served. Suddenly, he felt the urge to go – to take the
> bike and ride.

Activity 4

The verbs in the verb phrase do not always appear next to each other in
a sentence. Look at these sentences:

> **Would** you **like** some coffee?
> **Does** he always **take** sugar?

Identify the verb phrases in the following sentences:

1 Did you go to games on Tuesday?

2 Have you just bought a new pair of trainers?

Verbs and time

When we are writing or speaking, the events we describe can take place in either the **past**, the **present** or the **future**. We use verbs and other words to express past, present and future time.

Denzil **will play** for the school team	(refers to the **future**)
He **is** my only friend	(refers to the **present**)
Carol **had** all the luck	(refers to the **past**)

Activity 1

Identify the time referred to in these sentences:

 1 I <u>watched</u> television for ages because I <u>was</u> too <u>tired</u> to move!

 2 He <u>was hanging</u> around at the back of our house for a long time.

 3 Mum! Jane <u>has fallen over</u> in the garden!

 4 Mum! Jane <u>is lying</u> on the ground and she <u>is crying</u>.

 5 <u>Will</u> you <u>go</u> to Ben's party next weekend?

 6 We <u>had</u> a brilliant holiday in New Zealand.

 7 <u>Do</u> you <u>like</u> computer games?

 8 He <u>got</u> very angry when I <u>told</u> him about the incident.

 9 When <u>did</u> you last <u>see</u> her?

10 There <u>aren't</u> any spaces left, I'<u>m</u> afraid.

11 Paul <u>will be</u> in hospital for an operation next month.

Note

We often add suffixes to verbs to make them present or past:

verb	-ing	-ed
look	looking	looked
burn	burning	burned
call	calling	called

However, some verbs change the stem:

fall	falling	**fell**
buy	buying	**bought**
teach	teaching	**taught**

Verbs and time

Activity 2

Now let's try changing a passage from one time to another. Here is a short passage written in the past form:

> *I wondered what I should do next. Going to the police was out of the question, since they were unlikely to believe my story and I had no hard evidence. And, because he knew this, there wasn't any point in confronting Graham, either: if I did, he would simply deny it and laugh at me – or worse. At the time I couldn't see any way out.*

This is how it looks when written in the present:

> *I wonder what I should do next. Going to the police is out of the question, since they are unlikely to believe my story and I have no hard evidence. And, because he knows this, there isn't any point in confronting Graham, either: if I do, he will simply deny it and laugh at me – or worse. At the moment, I can't see any way out.*

1 Make a chart like the one below. Using the passages above, write down in column 1 the past tense form of each verb. In column 2 write down the present tense form of each verb.

Past	Present
Wondered	Wonder

2 What else has been changed in the second passage apart from the verbs? Why did this change have to be made?

Verbs and time

Activity 3

Here is another passage, written in the present:

Her tray is slippy in my hands as I lift it and chuck it against the wall. I bang my fists on the table and stand up; the table comes with me. I turn and kick myself free of it and the chair. I run round and pull down the boxes from the window ledges. The Lego pieces and the coloured straws scatter before me.

I bite the sleeve of my jumper. I can hear the ripping cloth. I whirl round.

There is something there in her eyes. Cloudy, shades of a sea storm. Pity? I take her handbag and empty it out onto her desk, then I hurl it at the blackboard. I grab some of the contents of her bag. Her personal things. Mirror, lipstick, comb. I smash them on the floor.

Her eyes are sharper now, bright with fear. And I am glad. It makes me stronger, exultant.

I wrench the classroom door open. I'm free. I'm running down the corridor, screaming.

1 Re-write the passage in the past tense.

2 Make a list of all the changes you have made.
You may notice some patterns in these changes. For example, you probably added the suffix **-ed** to some verbs to put them in the past tense. In how many cases did you have to add other letters, or change them?

3 The passage describes a very dramatic incident in a story. Decide whether its effect is more powerful in the present or the past tense, and explain why.

Verbs and time

Activity 4

It is important not to muddle time when writing. Inexperienced writers sometimes do this because they start in the past, then forget and drift into the present. Here is an example of tense 'drift':

> My mum shook me gently.
> 'Come on, you, it's 6.30, time to get up.'
> I groaned.
> 'You don't want to miss your holiday, do you?'
> That had me on my feet straight away, and I was soon down in the kitchen, with bare feet, still doing up my shirt buttons.
> Dad says, 'Hurry up and get your breakfast. I'll need your bag for packing in the boot in a few minutes.'
> I notice that it's a beautiful morning as I shovel down some cornflakes and wolf my way through three slices of toast and marmalade. Mum is filling flasks and arranging sandwiches in our big coolbox.

Re-write this passage, using either the present or the past tense throughout. Remember: it is easy to avoid muddling tenses if you check your writing as you go along.

Activity 5

Look back at some of your recent pieces of writing. Is each piece written in the past or the present? Are your tenses consistent?

Summary

Verbs are words or groups of words which express actions, emotions, thoughts and states of 'being' and 'having'.

Verb phrases can be one word or can be made up of a main verb and auxiliary verb(s).

When you are writing you must check to make sure your expression of 'time' is consistent.

Adverbs

Adverbs are words which provide the answers to these questions:

HOW?

WHEN?

WHERE?

Manjit walked **slowly** to school.	**adverb** tells us **how** Manjit walked
We went to a rave **yesterday**	**adverb** tells us **when** they went
It was **very** cold in the pool.	**adverb** tells us **how** cold it was
I put it **there**	**adverb** tells us **where** she put it.

We can combine two or three adverbs:

sarcastically tells us **how** she said it

She said it **really sarcastically**

really tells us **how** sarcastically

Identifying adverbs

1 Find the **verb(s)** in the sentence. For example:

John (ran) quickly with the ball.

2 The verb in the example is **ran**. Now ask yourself, '*When, where or how did John run?*' The sentence says he ran **quickly**, so the word *quickly* is the adverb.

3 You can often identify adverbs by finding words ending in **-ly**. Many adverbs are formed from adjectives by adding the suffix **-ly**.

graceful**ly**	thoughtful**ly**	tearful**ly**	thankful**ly**	slow**ly**	quick**ly**

However, do remember that many adverbs do *not* end in **-ly** e.g.:

tomorrow	soon	very	yesterday	there

Be careful: some words that end in **-ly** are *not* adverbs, such as *lovely*, which is an adjective.

Adverbs

Activity 1

Identify the **adverbs** in these sentences. Write them down.

1 She smiled cheerfully at her boyfriend.

2 I put the keys there.

3 My dad is coming here soon.

4 Dale was shaking terribly and muttering incoherently.

5 He slammed the glass down hard on the table.

6 The journey was mercifully short.

Activity 2

A reporter for the *Kilby Times* made these notes about a football match between Kilby Town and Grennon United:

F.A.Cup Round 3. Kilby Town 1, Grennon United 2.

Kilby start well. Webb runs at defence a lot. Breeze's header hits crossbar. After 15 mins, Grennon settle. Anderson passes to Drewitt for a goal for Grennon. Later, Campbell is fouled and scores from the kick for 2-0.

The reporter then wrote the following newspaper report based on her notes:

Town's early exit from cup

Kilby Town were soundly dumped out of the FA Cup yesterday by little Grennon United.

Kilby started brightly enough. Winger Tim Webb tormented the Grennon defence ceaselessly, and striker Mark Breeze saw a header thunder unluckily against the Grennon crossbar.

However, Grennon soon settled down, and after 15 minutes, Anderson threaded the ball neatly through to Drewitt, who ran through the Kilby defence to slot the ball past goalkeeper Chadney.

Campbell later added another for the visitors when he was cynically brought down as he sprinted towards the Kilby penalty area. He cleverly lobbed Chadney from the resultant free kick, and almost before Kilby could restart, the referee blew his half time whistle.

Adverbs

Activity 3

The writer's use of detail, and *adverbs* in particular, has brought the match to life for the reader. Write down all the adverbs that you can find in the report, including :

● *six* adverbs which tell you *how* something happened
● *two* adverbs which tell you *when* something happened.

Activity 4

Here are the notes on the second half of the game:

> After 10 minutes, Kilby pull a goal back – Webb pass to Mark Breeze. Good shot past Grennon goalkeeper Myers.
>
> Lots of pressure in last ten minutes. Richards hits the post (diving header); Eliot's shot from 25 yards well saved by Myers, but Grennon hold on.

1 From the notes, write the report of the second half. Try to maintain the *style* of the first part of the report. Use adverbs to make your writing lively.

2 Swap reports with a partner and underline all the adverbs.

Extension

Cut out a report of a football match from a newspaper. Do professional writers make much use of adverbs when writing their reports? Bring your report to school so you can compare different pieces.

Summary

Adverbs answer the questions:

● **How?**
● **When?**
● **Where?**

Your own writing

Activity

You are the casting director for a new TV drama mini-series on competitive sport. You've had some sketches drawn of the characters, but you want to send detailed written descriptions of their appearance, behaviour and personality to some actors' agencies.

Pardeep Singh
Football manager

Grant Razorbill
Rival football manager

Drago Hogweed
Groundsman

Storm O'Halloran
Marketing, publicity, design

Rodney Thunderbox
Goalkeeper

The basis of the plot is that Drago, Storm and Rodney are with Pardeep's team. Storm and Rodney often disagree, but will eventually fall in love. Drago, who has a secret criminal past, fancies Storm and hates Rodney. He will try to win her and ruin him. Grant Razorbill would like Storm to work for him and wants to wreck Pardeep's team because they are always winning.

Your task

Write a detailed description of each character. The agencies will use your description to find suitable actors and actresses. Aim to cover the following aspects:

- face (eyes, mouth, nose, complexion)
- height and build
- sound of voice and way of speaking
- general behaviour
- hair style and colour
- clothes
- the way the character moves
- personality.

You will need lots of **adjectives** (for characteristics) and **adverbs** (for the way they do things). When you have finished writing, circle all the adjectives and underline all the adverbs.

Examples:

Adjectives:	She has **blonde**, **flowing** hair. He is **spiteful**, **vicious** and **cruel**.
Adverbs:	He speaks **slowly** and **deliberately**. She walks **quickly** and **confidently**.

All change!

It is very important to understand that many words do not belong to just one class. The class in which we place a word depends upon what it is doing in a particular sentence. For example, take the word *shop*:

I usually **shop** for clothes on Saturday.	**shop is a verb** (tells you what the person does)
My favourite **shop** is Gap.	**shop is a noun** (name of a thing)

Activity 1

In each pair of sentences below, a word is used as a verb and as a noun. Say which is which.

1a The **test** was very hard.

1b They **test** new cars to make sure they are safe.

2a Jenny has a lovely **smile**.

2b I always **smile** when I think of her.

3a Can I **phone** you after 6pm tonight?

3b You can only use the **phone** during break and lunch time.

4a Tom learned to **ski** on a school trip.

4b Bond's left **ski** came off, so he balanced on the right one at 93mph while shooting the Russian soldiers behind him.

5a She found herself facing a huge black **dog** with hungry eyes.

5b Disaster seems to **dog** her everywhere she goes.

Activity 2

Here are some other words which can belong to the two classes, **noun** and **verb**:

beat
walk   **ship**
book   **try**

Write two sentences of your own for each word. In the first one, the word should act as a noun. In the second one, it should act as a verb.

Revision

Prefixes and Suffixes

1 **a** Write out the following words and underline the **prefix** in each
      word:

> defrost
>
> international
>
> unpack
>
> preview
>
> autobiography
>
> automatic

   b Write a sentence for each word to show how it could be used.

2 Write out each word in brackets and underline the **suffix** in each
     case:

   a The doctor (examined) the cut very (carefully).

   b We thought she had been (unfaithful) to her husband.

   c She looked so (helpless) after her mother died.

   d You behaved (disgracefully).

3 Write out the sentences below. Change the words in brackets into
     adverbs by adding the suffix **-ly**. Remember, you may need to change
     the spelling of the stem.

   a She thanked him very (sincere).

   b (Careful) the scientist examined the specimen.

   c She walked up to the teacher's desk (bold).

   d He looked tired and he spoke very (heavy).

   e (Busy) she sorted the cards into piles.

  If you need help look at pages 6–9.

Revision

Nouns

1 Write out the extract below and underline all the nouns.

> *Josh groped his way out of sleep, immediately
> remembering that the twins had a secret.
> Naturally, he didn't share it. He was always being
> left out now. But he was getting used to that, so
> why was he scared?*
>
> *He stumbled out of bed and pulled back the
> curtains, gazing at the broad sweep of the
> Thames at the bottom of the garden.*

2 Write out the plural of the following nouns:

address

glass   **church**

fox   **girl**   **vase**

buzz   **lady**

knife

chimney   **brush**

3 Write out the sentences below. Add apostrophes to the nouns in these
sentences *where necessary*. Some nouns are plural nouns which don't
possess anything, so don't need apostrophes.

  a We saw the girls in town last night.

  b I picked up the girls coat when it fell off her chair.

  c I found the gentlemans umbrella.

  d That is the cowards way out.

  e Someone had already put the knives on the table.

    If you need help look at pages 10–13.

Revision

Pronouns

1 Write out the passage below and replace some of the nouns with suitable pronouns:

> Alison left school early and hurried home to Alison's house. Alison had only half an hour to get changed and it was Alison's turn to wash the dishes and clean the house. Alison flicked a duster round the sitting room and ran the dishes quickly under the tap. Then Alison rushed upstairs to Alison's room. She had ten minutes to spare!

2 What type of pronoun is each underlined word below? Make a table like the one below and put the underlined words in column 1. In column 2 write down which type of pronoun it is.

   a <u>I</u> wish it wasn't <u>my</u> turn today.

   b <u>Whose</u> turn is it tomorrow?

   c I washed <u>myself</u> quickly.

   d <u>He</u> did his homework straight away when he came in from school.

   e I think the blue coat is <u>yours</u>.

Words	Type of pronoun
I	
My	

 If you need help look at pages 14–17.

Adjectives

1 Write down the passage below and underline all the adjectives.

> The river was a reassuring sight, calm and familiar, a slight haze rising from the surface in the early summer morning. The Thames was an old friend, always changing yet always the same, unlike the twins. They had a secret and they were afraid.

 If you need help look at pages 18–23.

Revision

Verbs

1 Write out the extract below and underline all the verb phrases. Remember verb phrases can be more than one word.

> *Jack and Tom seemed much closer than before. The way they looked at each other, whispered in their room, exchanged uneasy glances, seemed so obvious that he couldn't understand why Mum and Dad hadn't started to ask questions. But then they were so wrapped up in being busy, in getting edgy with each other, that Jack reckoned it wasn't so surprising they hadn't noticed.*

2 Now read the extract again and underline the auxiliary verbs in a different colour.

3 Rewrite the paragraph about Jack and Tom in the present tense.

 If you need help look at pages 24–32.

Adverbs

1 Choose adverbs from the box to fill the spaces in the sentences below. Write out your completed sentences.

> **afterwards**   **yesterday**   **thoughtfully**
> **well**   **quietly**

   a Talk _____ or you will wake the baby.

   b He frowned, then looked at Jason _____ .

   c He went home _____ .

   d We'd love you to come to the wedding and to the reception _____ .

   e Mix the ingredients together _____ .

2 Write out the sentences below. Underline the adverbs.

   a Damian whispered quietly in Sue's ear.

   b I checked my work carefully before handing it in.

   c I badly need a haircut.

   d He plays pool well.

   e Suddenly Donna realised she had left her bag behind.

   f I'll be ready soon.

   g Tomorrow I'm going to the dentist.

   h I have looked for the dog everywhere but I can't find him.

 If you need help look at pages 32–35.

Unit 3: Sentences

This unit helps you to understand more about how sentences work. Understanding more about sentences will enable you to reflect upon and improve your own writing.

a **Same again, Mike?**

b *Stop doing that!*

c *The smell of damp streets. Droning cars. A drunk belching beneath a bridge.*

d **Does God exist?**

e 'You OK?' **'HI!'** *'Yeah.'* **'Hello.'**

f The government yesterday won the first round of its battle to raise standards in schools, when the teaching unions and local education authorities rallied to support a White Paper promising hugely ambitious improvement targets and draconian penalties for underperformance.

Activity 1

With four or five other people, look at the groups of words on this page. Which groups of words would you say are sentences? Why?

What is a sentence?

Activity 2

Here are four rules which are sometimes used for identifying sentences:

> *1* A sentence must begin with a capital letter and end with a full stop, question mark or exclamation mark.
>
> *2* A sentence must have a verb.
>
> *3* A sentence is a string of words which makes sense.
>
> *4* A sentence sounds complete on its own.

1 Look at each rule in turn and see if it applies to all the groups of words on the opposite page.

2 Write out the four rules. After each one, write either *applies all the time* or *applies sometimes*.

Activity 3

Are the following groups of words sentences? Why/why not?

> **Bianca is a character EastEnders in.**

> **Home go.**

> **I'm going out tonight.**

Summary

You are able to identify that certain groups of words are sentences because sentences follow **patterns** we all recognise. In this unit you will learn about different types of sentences and the patterns they make. You will have noticed that it is possible to have really short sentences such as 'You OK?' and 'Sorry!'. As you work through this book you will learn that most sentences need a verb: '**Are** you OK?'.

Kinds of sentence

There are four main kinds of sentence:

Is he alive?	**He's dead.**	**What a mess!**	**Tell me who did it.**
Question	Statement	Exclamation	Command or request

Statement	These are the commonest kinds of sentences. Most sentences are statement sentences.
Question	If we want to find out the answer to something we ask a question. Question sentences have a different word order from statement sentences:

Is he dead? Question

He is dead. Statement

Many question sentences begin with 'Who...', 'What...', 'Which..', 'Is....', or 'How...'.

Exclamation	Exclamations say something surprising, exciting, urgent or awful.
Command or request	If we want someone to do something we make a command or request.

Activity 1

1 Read the extract from a play by Anne Fine on the opposite page. Identify:
   ● two statements   ● two questions   ● two exclamations.

2 What do the questions and exclamations tell us about the relationship between Kitty and Gerald?

3 Imagine that the next thing Gerald does is give Kitty a command. What might it be?

Kinds of sentence

from **The Play of Goggle Eyes**

Gerald is Kitty's mum's new boyfriend. He has just learned that Kitty's mum pays her for the odd jobs she does around the house.

Gerald And Kitty *charges* you for the potatoes!

Kitty's mouth drops open.

Kitty So? What's wrong with that?

Gerald What's wrong with that? I'll tell you what's wrong with it. It's simply appalling, that's what's wrong with it!

Kitty I don't see why.

Gerald Don't you?

Kitty No, I don't. It's not as if I were a bagsnatcher, or something. In fact, I think it's perfectly fair.

Gerald Perfectly fair? Why, it's truly disgusting!

Kitty abandons all attempts to stay polite.

Kitty Why? Why is it *(mocking him)* 'simply appalling' and 'truly disgusting'? I don't like gardening. Neither does Mum. It's a big chore. So now Dad's gone, Mum pays me for the vegetables, to keep me going.

Gerald What about you? Have you paid her yet for the lunch she's cooking and the bath she cleaned?

Mum But, Gerald, I'm her mother!

Gerald You are her *family*. And she is yours. You shouldn't be paying for her co-operation.

Activity 2

Work with a partner to write a very short playscript in which two characters argue. Write two versions, one in which the characters *only* speak in questions and one in which the characters *only* speak in statements. Then write a final version which contains a mixture of questions, statements, exclamations and commands.

You might write about:
- an argument with your parents or guardians because you want to go out somewhere they don't want you to go
- an argument with a friend who left you waiting for her for an hour.

Simple sentences

A simple sentence has one complete verb.

For example: Tim **played** tennis for Great Britain.

We can divide this sentence into different parts:

Tim + **played** + tennis + for Great Britain.

We can miss out parts of the sentence and still have a sentence which makes sense:

Tim **played** tennis.

Tim **played.**

But we can't miss out the verb:

Tim **tennis.**

Activity

1 The following newspaper report has lost its verbs! Choose verbs from the box below it to fit into each space. Remember, some verbs (or verb phrases) are more than one word. Write out the complete report.

80 die in fire horror at hotel

More than eighty people _____ yesterday in a massive hotel blaze. Many victims _____ behind fire doors. Flames and thick smoke_____through the 16-storey building. Several tourists _____ to their deaths from the top floor.
Others _____to safety by firemen.

perished   spread   were trapped   were taken   fell

2 A deadly scorpion has just escaped from the local zoo. It turns up in your school before it is caught.

Write a brief report about this incident for your local newspaper. Make your report really sensational.

Underline the verb phrases in your report.

The Subject

A simple sentence also has a subject:

The **ball** is red.

Subject

The subject usually tells us who or what the sentence is going to be about. It usually comes at the beginning of the sentence, before the verb:

Tom shut the window.
My mum likes *EastEnders*.
The tennis ball crashed through our neighbour's roof.

Activity 1

1 Identify the subjects in these sentences:

- Gemma is hoping to get a good school report next week.
- I am going to watch the Nice Girls in concert next Saturday.
- My dad wanted me to go shopping with him.

2 With a partner, think of subjects to fill the gaps in these sentences:

- _____ was very annoyed about her greenhouse.
- _____ goes to Judo every week.
- _____ go skating together every Friday.

The Subject

Activity 2

In the paragraph below the subjects have been mixed up. With a partner, work out where the subjects should go. Then write out the paragraph with the subjects in their proper places:

> **Gemma and Stuart** *is crumbling and grimy.* **The spooky old house** *lives there.* **Nobody** *is supposed to be haunted.* **The old house** *sneak in there to play sometimes.* **Gemma** *is very dark inside.* **It** *always runs away.*

It gets more complicated...

Sometimes the subject is not a person, people or thing(s):

> **It** was a cool September day.
> **There** was a robbery in the street last night.

Sometimes the subject does not come right at the beginning of the sentence:

> Next week, **Alison** is going to the cinema with Scott.
> Unfortunately, **they** forgot their tickets.

The Subject

Activity 3

Read the text below. Some sentences have their subjects in **bold**.
Other subjects have been left for you to identify:

> ***Darren Jones*** *was the last person to arrive at the hall. There
> was only one chair free. He sat down on the chair, which
> immediately collapsed with a loud splintering noise.
> Unfortunately, Darren's friends were standing over by the
> window.* ***They*** *exploded with laughter when they saw Darren
> lying in a heap on the floor. The red-faced boy picked himself
> up and headed for the door.*

Copy and complete the box below:

Sentence	The subject of this sentence is
The red-faced boy picked himself up and headed for the door.	
There was only one chair free.	
Unfortunately, Daniel's friends were standing over by the window.	

Extension

Look at the last sentence of the text in Activity 3. Rather than use the
subject 'Darren' again, the author has replaced the subject with words
giving us more information about Darren: **the red-faced boy**.

Find some examples of subjects in your recent writing.

Can you expand or replace some of your subjects with other words to
give the reader more information? For example:

● *The ship… The **sleek new flagship**…*

● *The boy… The **fair-haired** boy…*

Summary
   ● A simple sentence has one complete verb.
   ● A simple sentence has a **subject**.
   ● The subject usually tells us who or what the sentence is about.
   ● The subject usually appears at the beginning of the sentence *but not always*.
   ● The subject usually appears before the verb.
   ● The subject can be one word or a group of words – a phrase.

Checking agreement

One reason for learning to identify the subject in your sentences is to help you check that you are using the correct form of the verb.

> For example: I **was going** to the cinema.
> They **were going** to the cinema.
>
> In the first sentence the subject is I. In Standard English the verb which agrees with I is **was**. In the second sentence the subject is **They**. The verb which agrees with **They** is **were**.

Some teachers say that most of the mistakes in English writing are to do with misuse of the verbs **be** and **have**. So it is worth making sure you know the correct forms:

Subject	Verb		
	Have	**Be (Present)**	**Be (Past)**
I	have	am	was
he/she/it	has	is	was
we	have	are	were
you	have	are	were
they	have	are	were

Activity 1

Write out the correct forms of the sentences below:

1 We (was) the best in our school at swimming.

2 You (was) going to come to my house last night.

3 I (were) standing at the bus stop when I saw James.

4 James (were) with his friends, Mike and Tony.

Dialect

In some local dialects people might say '*I were*' and '*They was*'. There is nothing wrong with this when you are speaking in dialect but when you are writing in Standard English you should use correct Standard English forms.

Checking agreement

Problems with subjects

Most problems with subject/verb agreement occur when the subject is made up of more than one word:

> **Deborah and I** was shocked by what we saw.   ✗
>
> **Deborah and I** were shocked by what we saw.   ✓

Problems also occur when the subject is separated from the verb by another phrase:

> **My sister and her boyfriend**, Danny, someone she met at our school disco, was helping me with my homework.   ✗
>
> **My sister and her boyfriend**, Danny, someone she met at our school disco, were helping me with my homework.   ✓

Activity 2

Write out the following sentences. Change the verb in **bold** to make sure that the subjects and verbs agree.

1 The greatest interest in Tina's life **are** boys.

2 Jackie, who fell and sprained her ankle half way through the race, **were** last.

3 My dad and his best friend, whom I haven't seen for ages, **is** taking me to the Speedway tonight.

4 Everyone, except those who were late and those in detention, **are** being allowed the afternoon off.

Note: *Everyone* is singular so it behaves in the same way as *he/she/it*.

Summary

The **subject** and **verb** of a sentence should always agree with each other. It is always worth checking you have used the correct agreement in your written work:

1	Find the subject of your sentence.
2	Work out whether the subject of your sentence could be replaced by *I, you, we, they, she, he* or *it*.
3	Read the sentence to yourself with the correct pronoun in place of your subject and make sure you have the verb which matches it: **Deborah and I** were shocked → **we** were shocked.

Revision

Types of sentence

1 Write out each sentence below. Underneath each one, write whether it is a question, exclamation, statement or command.

   a There are some new houses being built close to our school.

   b Where are they building the new houses?

   c They're building new houses in the field at the end of the service road.

   d What a ridiculous thing to do!

   e Go and find out whether the building plans have been drawn up.

 If you need help look at page 44.

The simple sentence and the verb

2 Write out the sentences below. Underline the verb phrases.

   a The storm destroyed the ship.

   b My sister read three books last weekend.

   c I can't visit my grandmother in hospital this week.

   d We are going to the pictures.

   e Jason won his race yesterday.

   f Shall we go to France during the summer?

 If you need help look at page 46.

Extension

3 Write out the sentences below. Underline the verb phrases. Be careful – the words which make up the verb phrase do not always appear next to each other.

   a Would you like a drink?

   b What a fantastic colour your dress is!

   c I would like an ice-cream.

   d Do you like the Nice Girls?

   e She will have been waiting for ages.

   f I am going to go there by bus.

 If you need help look at pages 28 and 46.

Revision

The simple sentence and the subject

4 Write out the sentences below. Underline the subjects.

  a My mother is going to the parents' evening tonight.

  b The house cost a fortune.

  c I hope it will be a hot day tomorrow.

  d My brother and his wife are going to the Seychelles.

  e Cats love fish.

 If you need help look at page 47.

5 Write out the sentences below. Underline the subjects.

  a It was a beautiful sunny afternoon.

  b Yesterday, Alison had her hair cut.

  c The people who live next door have a really noisy dog.

  d Do you like the Nice Girls?

  e What a fantastic colour your dress is!

 If you need help look at pages 47–49.

Subject and verb agreement

1 Re-write these sentences so that the subjects and verbs agree. Some are correct so you need to decide which ones are wrong.

  a We was late again yesterday.

  b I were hoping to go home early but I was too busy.

  c My friends and I are going to see Newcastle play Sunderland next week.

  d Debbie, who is my best friend, and Theresa, who is the new girl in our class, is coming to my house tonight.

 If you need help look at pages 50–51.

In this unit we are going to look at how you can build sentences to make your writing more interesting. We will look at building simple sentences and then at how we form more complicated sentences.

Building simple sentences

First, a reminder: A simple sentence has one subject and one main verb.

Beginning parts	Subject	Verb	End parts
Yesterday	John	played	well.
	Some letters	arrived	today.

However, simple sentences needn't be short.
We can build simple sentences like this:

Some letters arrived today.

Some letters from all over the world arrived today.

Some brightly coloured letters of all sizes and from all over the world arrived today.

Jane spoke to a **strange woman.**

Jane spoke to a **very strange woman.**

Jane spoke to a **very strange woman with white hair.**

Jane spoke to a **very strange woman with bleached white hair.**

Vocabulary

We can describe the words in bold as **noun phrases**. This is because they act just like a single noun on its own.

Activity 1

Build the **bold** words in these sentences into noun phrases. The sentences will be used as parts of advertisements in your local paper:

    Ten **televisions** to be won!

    Buy this **bike** today!

Building noun phrases

Activity 2

Look at these pages from a picture book:

Grandpa was in the house.
He looked out of the window.
He saw a red car.
'Uncle Sami and Raza are here,'
he said.

3

Uncle Sami got out of the car.
A girl got out of the car too.
'This is Raza,' said Uncle Sami.
'She is your cousin.'

5

The editor of this book decided to produce a version for slightly older children. She changed the first sentence to read:

> *Grandpa was in the large old terraced house.*

Build the **bold** words in the following sentences into noun phrases to create a more detailed picture for the reader.

> He looked out of the **window**.   Uncle Sami got out of the **car**.

> A **girl** got out of the car too.

Activity 3

What is the effect of changing simple nouns to noun phrases? Can the added words improve the picture in your reader's mind?

1   Take one of your recent pieces of writing. Underline the single nouns in one colour and the noun phrases in another.

2   Try adding words to the nouns to make noun phrases which will help to build a better picture in your reader's mind.

Clauses

When we write simple sentences, they contain only one complete verb:

> I **went** to the pictures on Saturday.
>
> He **took** a picture of the sun setting behind the clouds.

However, we often write sentences that contain more than one complete verb:

> When I **went** to the pictures on Saturday I **took** my younger sister with me.
>
> He **took** a picture of the sun setting behind the clouds then **turned** to pack his suitcase.

These sentences are called **multiple sentences**. To understand how multiple sentences work we need to know about **clauses**.

Clauses

A clause is a group of words containing a complete verb. A simple sentence has just one clause.

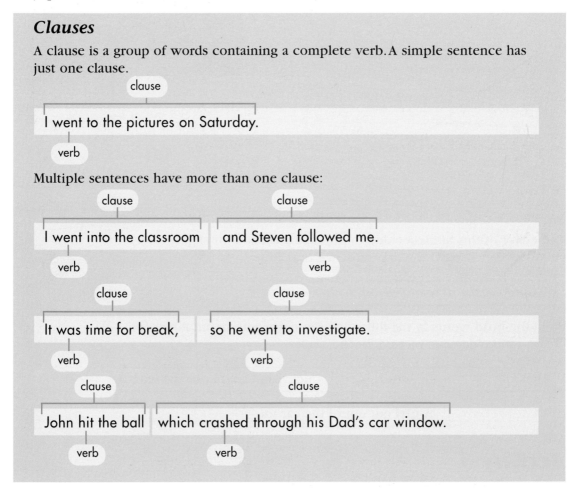

clause

I went to the pictures on Saturday.

verb

Multiple sentences have more than one clause:

clause — I went into the classroom — verb

clause — and Steven followed me. — verb

clause — It was time for break, — verb

clause — so he went to investigate. — verb

clause — John hit the ball — verb

clause — which crashed through his Dad's car window. — verb

You can also think of multiple sentences as sentences which have linking words:

linking word

I got up early this morning and I was late for work.

Clauses

Activity

Read the following text. It is taken from the beginning of an article about bullying:

When Schooldays Turn Into Nightmares

Andrew was always shy at school. He put on a lot of weight at the end of primary school and the other children started to tease him a bit. The trouble really started when he went to secondary school.

Andrew, now 13, was six months into his first year before his mother realised how badly he was being bullied.

'He wasn't very happy and he didn't seem to have any friends, but he'd always found it difficult to make them and I put it down to getting used to a new school. Then he came home with his blazer ripped. He told me he'd just tripped, which I believed to start with, as he had always been a clumsy child. Then he lost his bus pass three or four times. I got quite cross with him for being so careless yet Andrew still didn't want to admit anything was wrong at school.'

Work in pairs or groups for this activity.

1 Look closely at the text above. Find two examples of simple sentences. Remember, simple sentences have only one clause.

2 Find two examples of multiple sentences. Remember, multiple sentences have more than one clause. Look at the examples on the opposite page to help you.

Need help?

The easiest thing to do is to pick out the complete verbs in each sentence. If there is only one complete verb, it is a simple sentence. If there are two or more complete verbs, it is a multiple sentence.

Summary

- A **clause** is a part of a sentence which contains a complete verb.
- A **simple sentence** has only one clause.
- A **multiple sentence** has more than one clause.

Compound sentences

One type of multiple sentence is a **compound sentence**.
Compound sentences are what we get if we join two clauses together
with words such as **and**, **but**, **nor**, **then** and **yet**. Each part of the
compound sentence is equally important.

Simple sentence (or clause)

Janice liked the new album by Mush.
Polly got in the back of the car.
The first team played really well.

Simple sentence (or clause)

She couldn't afford to buy it.
Val drove.
They lost the match.

Compound sentence

Janice liked the new album by Mush **but** she couldn't afford to buy it.
Polly got in the back of the car **and** Val drove.
The first team played really well **yet** they lost the match.

Activity 1

| and | but | yet |

Join the simple sentences below using words from the box above:

1 He fell off his bike. He really hurt himself.
2 He fell off his bike. He didn't hurt himself.

3 Janice didn't do much work for English. She got a grade D in her exams.
4 Janice didn't do much work for English. She got a grade A in her exams.

5 Buy a new car at this low price. You'll never regret it.
6 Buy a new car at this low price. You'll live to regret it.

7 She's been playing the piano next door for two hours. It's driving me up the wall.
8 She's been playing the piano next door for two hours. I'm really enjoying it.

Vocabulary

Words which join sentences together such as **and**, **but** and **yet** are called
connectives or **conjunctions**.

Compound sentences: what goes wrong?

> I was walking home from school and I
> saw my friend, Mark, and he was out
> on his new bike and he asked me to go
> for a ride on it and I did and...

It is very easy to make your compound sentences longer and longer by adding more clauses to them linked by 'and' or 'but'. Such sentences can be tedious to read and make your writing very boring.

Activity 2

The following extract is from a story by a Year 9 student. The sentence is far too long. Try re-writing it without changing or removing any words except *and* and *but*.

> We arrived at 9.30 and found the party in full swing and Katy was already there with Clive and Jayne and Gemma was sitting with her new boyfriend, Alan, on the sofa, but we couldn't see any of our other friends and we made our way through the packed sitting room to the kitchen and there wasn't much left to eat and David offered to go to the shop.

Connectives

Sentences are often joined together with **connectives** such as *and* or *but* (see pages 58–59). However, your writing will be more interesting if you use a variety of connectives, such as:

after	because	so	though	where	who
although	if	since	until	which	yet
as	or	then	when	while	

Activity 1

Choose connectives from the box above and write out the following sentences, completing the gaps. Try not to use a connective more than once. The first one has been done for you.

1 There was no bus for an hour **so** we decided to take a taxi.

2 She carried on running _____ she had sprained her ankle.

3 He couldn't get the hang of it _____ I had explained the rules again.

4 Everybody was there by 1p.m. _____ the game didn't start until 2.45.

5 Warren slipped inside and took the papers _____ Sheila created a diversion.

6 My parents have grounded me _____ I stayed out until 3a.m.

7 I borrowed Julie's racquet _____ it was better than mine.

8 I haven't been able to play football _____ I sprained my ankle two weeks ago.

9 You can tidy your room _____ you have finished your dinner.

Your own writing

Look carefully at some examples of your own recent writing. Underline the connectives you use. Could you improve your writing by using a greater variety of connectives?

Connectives

Turning sentences around

Look again at the nine sentences on the previous page. Each one is made of two sentences joined by a connective:

> You can go and tidy your room **when** you have finished your dinner.

Some of these sentences can be reversed. For example:

> **When** you have finished your dinner, you can go and tidy your room.

Notice that we put a comma between the two halves.

Activity 2

1 Look at the nine sentences on the previous page and work out which ones can be reversed.

2 Write out the reversed versions of the sentences you have picked out.

Activity 3

Work with a partner for this activity.

Using the connectives listed on the previous page, join the following pairs of sentences together.

Try not to use a connective more than once. Reverse the order of at least three of the sentence pairs.

1 He was brought down by a sliding tackle. He was taken to hospital with a broken leg.

2 They were hoping to go for a picnic. It poured with rain all day.

3 I showed him how to do it. He made a complete mess of the whole thing.

4 Mum opened the bonnet and checked the electrics. Dad went to telephone the AA.

5 Make sure you are there on time. You will not get a seat.

6 He was feeling sick. Darren went to the party anyway.

7 They found Darren unconscious in the bathroom. They had been looking for him for ten minutes.

8 She doesn't buy a lot of new clothes. She's saving up for a tool set.

Complex sentences

The sentences you made in your work on using connectives (pages 60–61) are examples of **complex sentences**.

Complex sentences are another type of **multiple sentence**. Complex sentences have more than one clause. The clauses can be combined in several different ways.

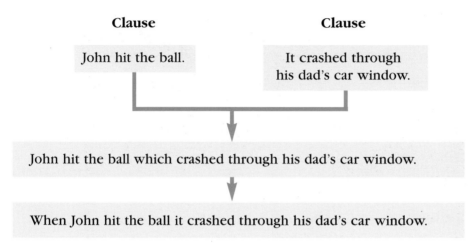

Clause	Clause
John hit the ball.	It crashed through his dad's car window.

John hit the ball which crashed through his dad's car window.

When John hit the ball it crashed through his dad's car window.

Main and subordinate clauses

Main clauses can stand on their own.

Main clause	Main clause
John hit the ball.	It crashed through his dad's car window.

Subordinate clauses need to be joined to a **main clause.**

Main clause	Subordinate clause
John hit the ball	which crashed through his dad's car window.

Here is another example:

Main clause	Subordinate clause
She slipped over on a spilt drink	while she was dancing.

Complex Sentences

Activity

The left-hand column below contains main clauses. Next to each one in the right-hand column is a subordinate clause, but not the right one: the column has been jumbled up.

Match the main clauses on the left with their subordinate clauses on the right and write out the complete sentences:

1 Daniel tried on fifteen pairs of shoes	**a** while he shouted 'You'll never catch me!'
2 The plumber came this morning	**b** while he was in the shop.
3 We're going to Ibiza in July	**c** after three socks and a half-eaten sandwich got stuck in the vacuum cleaner.
4 Ellie broke her shoe	**d** since he was about to be attacked by a man-eating spider.
5 I'm going out with Billy tonight	**e** if Mum manages to book the flight.
6 Have you seen Tina's book	**f** which she left on top of the radiator?
7 Pam chased Robbie round the kitchen	**g** but she couldn't find the stopcock.
8 Mum forced me to tidy my room	**h** when Tom arrived with his friends.
9 He thought it might be best to run	**i** as she walked home from the party.
10 I was getting ready to go out	**j** even though I finished with him last week.

What do you notice about the words at the beginning of the subordinate clauses?
What type of words are they? Look back at pages 58–61 if you need help.

More about clauses

Sometimes the main clause appears at the beginning of the sentence. At other times the subordinate clause appears at the beginning of the sentence.

In these examples, the main clause is in **bold**. The subordinate clause is in colour.

> **Her giant poster of Manchester United fell off the wall** while she was asleep.

> While she was asleep, **her giant poster of Manchester United fell off the wall.**

> **I stayed up late to finish my homework** although I was tired.

> Although I was tired, **I stayed up late to finish my homework.**

> Even though our striker was brilliant, **our team lost the match.**

> **Our team lost the match** even though our striker was brilliant.

Notice that, if the subordinate clause comes first in a sentence, it needs to be followed by a comma.

Activity 1

In pairs, join clauses 1–5 at the top of the next page to make complex sentences.

You need to decide which clause is to be the subordinate one, which connective to use and where to put it.

Try to put subordinate clauses at the beginning of at least two of the sentences.

> **Example**
>
> Penny was late for the third time this week. Mr Edwards put Penny in detention.
>
> *Solutions*
>
> Since Penny was late for the third time this week, **Mr Edwards put her in detention.**
>
> *or*
>
> **Mr Edwards put Penny in detention** because she was late for the third time this week.
>
> Notice that you can change the subject (e.g. *Penny*) into a pronoun (e.g. *she, her*) to make the sentence flow more smoothly.

More about clauses

1 James passed to Carlo. Carlo blasted the ball to the back of the net.

2 We're not speaking to each other. Alison was rude about my mum's pink and green hair.

3 I've only been playing hockey for two months. I scored twice in the match on Wednesday.

4 On Saturday we had lunch at Burger Queen. Burger Queen is my favourite restaurant.

5 My mum dropped a hammer on Dad's head. They were trying to put up a picture.

Activity 2

Now compare your sentences with those of other pairs in your group. How many different variations did you make?

Summary

- A **multiple sentence** has more than one clause.
- A **compound sentence** joins two clauses using the connectives **and**, **but**, **or**, **nor**, **then**, **yet**.
- A **complex sentence** combines clauses in different ways.

A main clause can stand on its own: *Mum forced me to tidy my room.*

A subordinate clause cannot stand on its own because it is incomplete: *...even though I finished with him last week.*
...when Tom arrived with his friends.

Subordinate clauses begin with **connectives.**

Sentences and how to stop them

A common mistake in students' writing is to join two clauses using only a comma.

For example, here are two clauses: **John got up. He put on his clothes.**

Some students write: **John got up, he put on his clothes.**

Joining sentences in this way leads to rambling, confusing sentences which are difficult to read.

Look at this passage:

> *The alarm went off, John woke up, he turned over with a groan, the smell of frying bacon drifted into the room, he became conscious of his hunger, he'd eaten nothing since Sunday lunch. He knew it was late, his dad was cooking the breakfast, he had to get to the works by 9.00, he rolled away from the wall he hauled himself out of bed, he began to pull on his clothes.*

- The passage consists of two long rambling sentences.
- The word **he** is repeated too many times.
- You don't know whether it's John or his dad who has to be at the works at 9.00: the repeated use of **he** makes the sentence confusing.

Here is the passage again, with better use of punctuation and conjunctions:

> *The alarm went off. John woke up and turned over with a groan. As the smell of frying bacon drifted into the room, he became conscious of his hunger. He'd eaten nothing since Sunday lunch. Also, he knew it was late because his dad, who had to get to the works by 9.00, was cooking the breakfast. He rolled away from the wall, hauled himself out of bed and began to pull on his clothes.*

- The length of the sentences is varied.
- The meaning is clear (for example, we know that it's John's **dad** who has to be at the works by 9.00).

> **Hint:** To decide where your own sentences should stop, try reading your work onto tape. Listen to the tape and notice where you pause naturally. Should there be a full stop where you pause?

Sentences and how to stop them

Activity

Re-write this passage, adding connectives and full stops as necessary. Use the connectives box on page 60 to help you.

Try to vary the sentence lengths, and avoid too much repetition of he or she. Also, make sure it is clear *who* is doing *what*.

Sam rode his bike over to Fairfield, he was joined at the rec. by Alan, he was on his new mountain bike, it had servo-assisted gear selection and anti-lock brakes. He couldn't stop boasting about it, Tracey arrived she challenged him to a race up and down the old mounds of earth and debris, they had been left by the builders of the estate. Alan said it was always a pleasure to give a girl a good thrashing, he charged off up the first muddy slope, his back wheel spun furiously, Sam was covered in mud from head to foot. Tracey was soon in hot pursuit and catching up, she was a brilliant rider she knew all the tricks, Alan's super-fast gear changer gave him an advantage. He managed to hold her off, their bikes slithered and slewed through the thick black mud, great sprays of it shot high in the air, Alan was so excited he didn't even care about his new Nike Airs, they were plastered with mud. He came to the top of the last mound at high speed, the bike took off, he was caught off guard, he leaned back, the bike did a back somersault, he was hurled off sideways into the filthy stagnant ditch alongside the path. The back wheel of the bike bounced off a rock at the bottom, the bike careered into a high garden wall, there was a terrible sound of buckling metal and splintering plastic.

Your own writing

Activity

Describe the sequence of pictures below. Try to use a variety of different sentences in your description.

Looking at a text

Activity

This advert appeared in several national newspapers. Read it carefully.

They took his teeth.
They took his claws.
Now they're going for his throat.

This bear, like many others in Pakistan, is being set upon by savage dogs as a spectator sport.

His teeth and claws have been pulled out and his nose drilled through to accommodate a rope.

And to make things even more unfair, he is tethered to the ground during the fight.

As part of the World Society for the Protection of Animals, the Libearty Campaign is dedicated to stamping out this illegal activity.

Bear-baiting is barbaric.

Just £5 will help us enforce the law and bring the cruelty to a stop.

World Society for the Protection of Animals

1 What is this advert about? What is it asking you to do?

2 Which sentences in the advert are simple sentences?

3 What patterns can you see in the simple sentences?

4 Why do you think the authors have used simple sentences in this way? What impact do they have?

Revision

Noun phrases

1 Write out the following sentences and underline the noun phrases in each one.

   a The sleek black cat caught the bird.

   b The woman with dark hair came out of the mysterious old house.

   c A brown and white dog ran across the busy road in front of a fast car.

   d The nervous man coughed and stammered before he made his speech.

   e Shattered glass and broken locks greeted the couple when they returned from their holiday.

 If you need help look at pages 54–55.

Simple, Compound and Complex Sentences

2 Which of the following sentences are simple, compound or complex?

   a I made the dinner last night.

   b I arrived home late because I had been talking to Alison.

   c I really wanted to come to the party but John was too tired.

   d The man had long red hair tied in a pony tail and was driving a red Ford Fiesta.

   e Have you seen the new car yet?

   f After I heard my dad had won the lottery, I couldn't concentrate on any school work at all.

   g The car skidded round the corner and crashed straight into our garden wall.

 If you need help look at pages 56–65.

3 Turn each group of simple sentences into a multiple sentence. Your multiple sentences can be compound or complex sentences.

   a My sister dropped the vase. It had been in our family for years.

   b I woke up really late yesterday morning. I managed to get to school on time.

   c Tim woke up really early yesterday morning. He saw an amazing sunrise.

   d They finally arrived at the camp site. They were exhausted. They had spent five hours driving round Cornwall trying to find the right place.

 If you need help look at pages 56–65.

In this unit we will look at some parts of the sentence not yet covered in the book. This unit will give you a better understanding of how sentences work as a whole.

Parts of a sentence

We learned in Unit 3 that:

● simple sentences follow patterns   ● simple sentences have a subject and a verb.

Subject	Verb	
He	dropped	the ball.
The people next door	like	going to the pictures.
Alison	is	my sister.

Some other parts of the sentence are:

Object

In a simple statement sentence the object usually comes after the verb. The object tells you who or what has been directly affected by the action of the verb.

He dropped	**the ball.**	> Object
He has been looking after	**her cat.**	

Some verbs like *come* and *arrive* do not take objects. To help you check which verbs take objects, use the following sentence. If you can put a verb in the blank, then it can take an object:

I _____ this thing.

Subject complement

Like the object, the subject complement usually comes after the verb. However, while the object and the subject are different things, the subject complement 'completes' the subject by telling us more about it.

Alison is	**my sister.**	> Subject complement
I am	**very angry.**	

Compare these sentences:

Mr Black met	**our sister.**	— Object
Mr Black is	**our teacher.**	— Subject complement

Object and Complement

Activity 1

1 Write out these sentences and underline the object in each of them:

   a Tom hates the doctor.

   b Paul broke the snooker table.

   c They played an exciting game of tennis.

   d Janice bought a fantastic mountain bike yesterday with loads of gears.

2 Write out these sentences and add an object to each of them:

   a Jake threw _____ .

   b I really want _____ .

   c Joanne plays _____ every Thursday at the sports club.

Activity 2

In groups, imagine that you are journalists at *The Scum* newspaper. It is your job this week to dream up some punchy headlines.

All of your headlines are to follow a **subject–verb–object** pattern, for example:

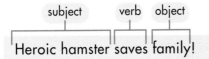

The first person in your group dreams up a subject. The next person adds the verb. The next person adds the object.

See how many way-out headlines you can create!

Activity 3

Write out the following sentences and underline the subject complements:

1 She looked happy.

2 Ken is captain of the football team.

3 Jane is a beautiful girl.

Adverbial phrases

Another part of the sentence is the **adverbial** or **adverbial phrase**.
The adverbial phrase answers questions such as: **When? Where? How?**

Subject	Verb	Adverbial
He	left	at five o' clock.
They	walked	very slowly.
I	am leaving	tomorrow morning.
The car	was swerving	all over the place.

Activity

Write out the following sentences and underline the adverbial phrase in each one:

1 My girlfriend telephoned me last night.

2 James scowled with great ferocity.

3 The lorry swerved in a very unstable way.

4 Slowly, she walked across the room.

5 Next year, we're going to win the league.

A useful reminder: phrases and clauses

Phrase

In this book you have come across the term *phrase* several times. A phrase is a group of words that work together. We have looked at:

Verb phrases	I **should be going** home soon.
Noun phrases	**The beautiful golden-haired child** smiled at me.
Adverbial phrases	Tim was driving **very slowly**.

Clause

A *clause* is a group of words containing a complete verb. A sentence contains at least one clause.

A **simple sentence** contains only one clause. This is both a simple sentence and a clause:

> I went home at midnight.

A **multiple sentence** contains more than one clause:

> I went home at midnight and got up for work at 6.00 the next morning.

> Although I went home at midnight, I got up for work at 6.00 the next morning.

The different kinds of sentences we write need to be grouped and linked together to make a complete **text**. This grouping and linking is called **paragraphing**.

Well-planned paragraphs are like properly made sentences: they make it easy for the reader to follow what you are trying to say. Paragraphs achieve this in two ways:

1 They break up the text so that it's not a solid block on the page. Paragraphs with spaces between them *look* more inviting to the reader than a spaceless mass of words, which just puts people off.

Compare the two pages on the right. The top one has paragraphs with plenty of space between, so that you don't feel hemmed in. These divisions also make it easier for you to keep your place. If you lost it while reading the bottom page, you would have great difficulty finding it again among the mass of words. Also, the big block of text *looks* like hard work!

2 Paragraphs are signals to the reader: when you start a new one, she or he knows that you are moving from one stage in your text to another.

> Her tray is slippy in my hands as I lift it and chuck it against the wall. I bang my fists on the table and stand up; the table comes with me. I turn and kick myself free of it and the chair. I run round and pull down the boxes from the window ledges. The lego pieces and the coloured straws scatter before me.
>
> I bite the sleeve of my jumper. I can hear the ripping cloth. I whirl round.
>
> There is something there in her eyes. Cloudy, shades of a sea storm. Pity? I take her handbag and empty it out onto her desk, then I hurl it at the blackboard. I grab some of the contents of her bag. Her personal things. Mirror, lipstick, comb. I smash them on the floor.
>
> Her eyes are sharper now, bright with fear. And I am glad. It makes me stronger, exultant.

> Her tray is slippy in my hands as I lift it and chuck it against the wall. I bang my fists on the table and stand up; the table comes with me. I turn and kick myself free of it and the chair. I run round and pull down the boxes from the window ledges. The lego pieces and the coloured straws scatter before me. I bite the sleeve of my jumper. I can hear the ripping cloth. I whirl round. There is something there in her eyes. Cloudy, shades of a sea storm. Pity? I take her handbag and empty it out onto her desk, then I hurl it at the blackboard. I grab some of the contents of her bag. Her personal things. Mirror, lipstick, comb. I smash them on the floor. Her eyes are sharper now, bright with fear. And I am glad. It makes me stronger, exultant. I wrench the classroom door open. I'm free. I'm running down the corridor, screaming.

Let's look at the beginning of a story to see how starting a new paragraph can signal a change.

Vivien Alcock has written a story which begins like this:

> *Barbara Heston is the most important person in our class. She is a large girl with a loud voice, curly red hair and big white teeth. Her friends say she is pretty. If you're small, you keep out of her way.*
>
> *The new girl was small. Her name was Lily Barnes, though she looked more like a weed than a lily, being thin and nervous, as if she was afraid some gardener would come and yank her out by the roots and throw her on the rubbish heap. She was wearing the wrong clothes.*

Using paragraphs

Vivien had pictures in her mind of the two main characters in her story, the bully and the victim. She decided to start by describing them, so that her readers could share the pictures and understand what follows in the story.

She wrote first about the bully, Barbara. Then, when starting to describe Lily, she also started a new **paragraph**. This is a visual signal to her readers that she is moving from one subject – Barbara – to her next subject – Lily.

Activity 1

The two pictures below illustrate the opening of a story about a fishing trip:

Write the first two paragraphs of the story, concentrating on what happens and when, rather than on the personalities of the characters. Here is a list of the things you could include in each paragraph:

Paragraph 1

● what Tom is doing

● the time

● what Tom is carrying

● the weather and how it makes Tom feel.

Paragraph 2

● what Sharon is doing

● what Sharon has with her

● the time Tom arrives at the bus stop

● how Sharon reacts when she sees him.

Linking paragraphs

Activity 2

A local hotel has employed some weekend workers to help with the catering. You are in charge of making sure they know how to prepare the morning tea and toast just how the guests like it.

Write a set of instructions for making and serving the toast. You should order and link your paragraphs so they are easy to follow. Here are some of the steps you should cover.

- cutting bread straight
- cutting bread to size which fits toaster slots
- setting brownness control before pushing down lever
- keeping an eye on toaster in case of burning
- being careful not to burn fingers on hot toast
- spreading jam after butter if required
- serving with hot tea or coffee

Write your instructions using a new paragraph for each subject.

For each paragraph, you should try to start with a word or phrase which leads the reader in from the paragraph before, but avoid using the same word or phrase twice. Some suggestions are given in the boxes below.

First paragraph	Middle paragraph	
First of all…	Next…	Then…
To start with…	The second stage is…	Your next task
The first step is…	After…	Following…
The process begins with…		For the next stage…

Last paragraph
To finish the job…
Finally…
As a final touch…
Lastly…

Finally, redraft your toast-making instructions.

Sequencing

In the previous sections we have arranged and linked paragraphs in a way which helps the reader's understanding. In this section, we're going to practise arranging paragraphs to make a complete story or text.

Activity 1

The numbered paragraphs below make up the **autobiography** (a life story written by the person concerned) of the writer Vivien Alcock. However, they are mixed up. See if you can work out a sensible order for them.

1 After the war, I worked as a commercial artist for several years, only stopping when our daughter Jane was born. Telling her bedtime stories awakened my interest in writing again and that is how I began.

2 I was born in Worthing, Sussex, the youngest of three sisters. We were seaside children, with sand between our toes and our rooms filled with drying seaweed and shells and coloured pebbles. In summer, we played for hours on the beach. In winter, we would dress up in mackintoshes, sou'westers and gumboots and go and watch the waves crashing against the sea wall, throwing up fountains of spray high above our heads.

3 I only once came across a school bully, in a school whose name I have happily forgotten. She didn't think much of me. She told me so the first day.

4 Our mother was ill for as long as I can remember, and I think this drew the three of us closer together. We were all fond of painting and reading, and used to tell each other bedtime stories. As I was the youngest, my turn came last, and before I had properly begun, my sisters would be fast asleep. I think this is what made me want to be a writer. I was determined to get my stories told at last.

Your writing

5 For some reason, before I was twelve, we kept changing schools. This meant we were often new girls, coming into our different classes where everyone else had been together for ages – always difficult if you're shy.

6 After school, I studied at the Oxford School of Art, intending to be a teacher, but I volunteered for the army before I had finished my course. This was at the time of the Second World War. I became an ambulance driver, serving in France, Belgium and Germany. My husband, Leon Garfield, was in the Medical Corps, and we met in an army canteen in Belgium.

Activity 2

The boxes on the next page contain facts about the life of the writer Robert Swindells, in no particular order. Using your experience from the previous activity, try writing his **biography** (life story written by someone else).

Here are some notes to help you:

● Since you are writing about someone else, you need to use '**he**', not '**I**'.

● Although the facts have been grouped, you don't *have* to follow the groupings. Nor do you have to make one paragraph for each group.

● The key to doing well here is to **plan your writing in advance**:

   1 decide on an **order** for the facts (e.g. will you start with his birth, or with the fact that he didn't want to be a writer?)

   2 put the facts in order, then group them as seems sensible to you

   3 use each of your fact groups as a basis for writing one paragraph of text.

Your writing

Robert Swindells

- after war, no gas masks – used the case to hold packed lunch
- lunch: jam buttie, with cod-liver oil and orange juice

- didn't want to be a writer
- wanted to be either a Spitfire pilot or a red deer stag
- tried many jobs – ended up as a writer
- Mr Gledhill may have been right
- two favourites among his own books:
  The Ghost Messengers
  Room 13

- two school memories:
  1 truants from another school threw dead cat through open window during Miss Lewis's Divinity lesson
  2 Mr Gledhill, English teacher – liked Robert's stories, said he might make a writer.

- once older, no more orange juice
- only liked two things at school:
  1 English
  2 Going home
- failed eleven-plus exam and left school at fifteen

- headmistress of primary school came into classroom one day to say war (Second World War) was over – she was crying
- surprising – had never seen adult cry before
- headmistress said they could go home
- on way home, women laughing, crying, hugging each other
- Robert scared: had adults gone barmy?

- born in Bradford, 1939
- started school 1944, aged 5
- war on: each pupil had peg on classroom wall for gas mask
- had gas drill and shelter drill
- too young to understand it all

Summary
- **Paragraphs** group and link your sentences into a complete text.
- Paragraphs break up your text into sections so that it is easy to read. They indicate to your reader that you are moving from one stage of your text to another.
- Paragraphs should be linked and sequenced so that your text flows and is in a logical order.

Unit 7: Punctuation

 This unit shows you how to punctuate your work correctly. You can use it for reference or work through each section using the activities for practice. When your teacher picks up a mistake in your punctuation, work through the relevant section and use the activities to make sure you get it right next time.

Capital letters

You are probably familiar with some uses of capital letters. The most common uses are:

1 To begin every sentence.

2 To begin every new speech (see pages 90–91):

> David said angrily, 'You should have taken more care.'

3 For the personal pronoun 'I'.

4 For the names or titles of:

People	Countries	Companies
Mr Jones	Northern Ireland	Nike
Jim Carrey	Russia	Ford
Camilla Parker Bowles	New Zealand	Safeway

Products	Places	Books, films, TV programmes and so on
Doc Martens	London	The Shining
Frosties	East Timor	Brookside
Coke	Beijing	Charlie and the Chocolate Factory

You should also use capital letters for:

5 The names of days and months:

Monday	Tuesday	January	February

6 Names of political parties, religious faiths, organizations:

Labour	Catholic	Department for Education
Conservative	Protestant	Trading Standards Authority

7 Abbreviations of words which would begin with a capital letter if written in full:

BBC	J. A. Smith	N Ireland	SW England

Capital letters

Capital letters are not needed for

Standard compass points:

| north | east | south | west |

The seasons:

| spring | summer | autumn | winter |

Activity

The text below was typed by a newspaper reporter. Unfortunately the keyboard was not working properly, so he could not use capital letters. See if you can re-write it with capital letters in the right place.

car clamper rises to new heights

alan pearman, a wheelclamp official, was left dangling yesterday. he and his car were hoisted 10 feet in the air by a fork-lift truck.

it happened after mr pearman, 27, clamped a saab car on torquay harbourside. it belonged to a crane driver steve carter, 40.

mr carter's boss, john thompson, hoisted mr pearman's fiesta van aloft – with him inside. he claimed that mr carter's car was parked legally in the company's parking space.

mr thompson said: 'i was so angry that if the forklift hadn't jammed, i'd have dumped him in the harbour.'

the department of transport commented: 'the owner of the vehicle should have displayed his parking permit where it could easily be seen. there have been a number of illegally parked cars this winter and we need to crack down on it.'

the independent, friday 3 jan 1992

Full stops, Question marks and Exclamation marks

At the end of every sentence, you should always place one of these three marks:

| full stop | . | question mark | ? | exclamation mark | ! |

Which one you need depends on the type of sentence you are writing:

	Type of sentence
Burger Queen is my favourite restaurant. –	Statement
What are you doing? –	Question
Stop that at once, you idiot! –	Exclamation

Full stops

Full stops are used:

1 At the end of a statement sentence.

2 In abbreviations which do not end with the same letter as the full form of the word:

So: February ⟶ Feb.
Reverend ⟶ Rev.

But: Doctor ⟶ Dr
Reverend ⟶ Revd

Question marks

Question marks are needed for **direct** questions:

1 A straightforward question:

What are you doing tonight?

2 Where a question is quoted word-for-word:

He asked me, 'Where do you come from?' – Direct question

Statement   Question

Question marks are not needed for **indirect** questions, where the question is reported rather than asked directly:

He asked me where I came from. – Indirect question

Statement

When writing, be careful not to mix the two kinds of question:

He asked me where do I come from?   X

This does not make sense: it is a mixture of a statement and a question.

Question marks are easy to forget, so always check your writing to make sure that you have put them in where needed.

Full stops, Question marks and Exclamation marks

Exclamation marks

Only use exclamation marks when someone shouts, cries out, gives an order or says something very forcefully:

Avoid sprinkling exclamation marks throughout your writing in an attempt to amuse, as it becomes annoying to read and loses its impact:

> *Hi, Jane!! How are you getting on?!!! Was the holiday really brill?!! I bet you're really brown – I'll be dead jealous!!!!!*

Activity

Punctuate the following passages correctly, putting in full stops, question marks and exclamation marks where necessary. You do not need to add any commas.

> As we all climbed into the car, our excitement was so intense we could hardly bear it
>
> 'How fast will it go' we cried out 'Will it do fifty miles an hour'
>
> It'll do sixty' she answered Her tone was so confident and cocky it should have scared us to death, but it didn't
>
> 'Oh, let's make it do sixty' we shouted 'Will you promise to take us up to sixty'
>
> 'We shall probably go faster than that,' she announced, pulling on her driving-gloves and tying a scarf over her head in the approved driving-fashion of the period
>
> We were all quivering with fear and joy as the driver let out the clutch and the great long black automobile leaned forward and stole into motion
>
> 'Are you sure you know how to do it' we shouted 'Do you know where the brakes are'
>
> 'Be quiet' she snapped 'I've got to concentrate'

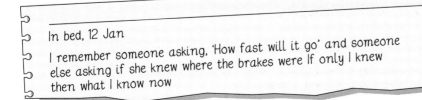

In bed, 12 Jan

I remember someone asking, 'How fast will it go' and someone else asking if she knew where the brakes were If only I knew then what I know now

Commas

How you use commas in your writing is often up to you. It depends upon the style of writing you want to use. However, commas should be used:

1 To separate the items in a list:

> I'd like the steak with rice, green peas, beans and carrots.
> Afterwards I'd like grapes, strawberries, bananas and ice-cream.

Notice that you don't need a comma before 'and' in the list.

2 To separate direct speech from the words which introduce or follow it:

> Peter said, 'Give me back my ferret.'
> 'Not until I've rescued it from my trousers,' said James.

Commas are not needed in the address, date, opening or closing salutations of business letters:

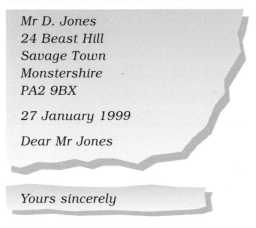

Mr D. Jones
24 Beast Hill
Savage Town
Monstershire
PA2 9BX

27 January 1999

Dear Mr Jones

Yours sincerely

Commas are not needed, either, before speech marks around titles: *The film was called 'Lawrence of Arabia'.*

Activity 1

The following sentences have commas missing. Write out the sentences, putting in the commas where they belong.

1 I liked Miss Watkins. She was impatient intelligent generous and interesting.

2 Major Collins was boring mean arrogant and unkind.

3 I opened the door and Richard said 'Did you get my message?'

4 'If you had let me know earlier it would have been better' I replied.

5 'I did try to phone you' Richard explained 'but there was no answer.'

6 'Well' I said 'now you are here I hope you have brought the rolls sausages ketchup and burgers for the barbecue.'

Commas

You should also use commas to separate different parts of a sentence.

1 Where a subordinate clause comes before the main clause, a comma should separate them:

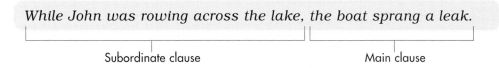

While John was rowing across the lake, the boat sprang a leak.

Subordinate clause   Main clause

2 A comma should come at the end of each main clause in a longer sentence unless the next clause begins with a connective (*and*, *but* and so on):

Main clause   Main clause

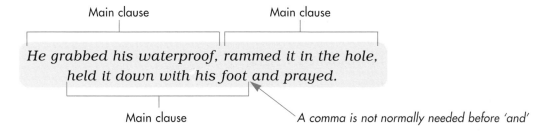

He grabbed his waterproof, rammed it in the hole, held it down with his foot and prayed.

Main clause   A comma is not normally needed before 'and'

3 Where a subordinate clause is placed in the middle of a sentence, a comma should be used on either side of it:

Main clause   Subordinate clause

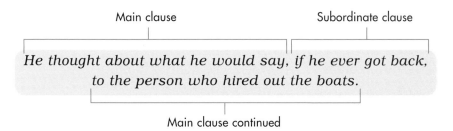

He thought about what he would say, if he ever got back, to the person who hired out the boats.

Main clause continued

Activity 2

Write out the following sentences, putting in commas where you think they should go:

1 After what seemed a lifetime I saw him at last.

2 He was wearing a shabby old bomber jacket faded blue jeans a pair of old trainers and was carrying his helmet.

3 I was about to go up to him if only my courage would hold out and warn him about the others.

4 Just before I reached him he swung round put his helmet on the counter ordered a coffee and then headed towards the payphone.

Apostrophes

Apostrophes have two main uses:

1 To show that a letter has been missed out in order to shorten a word:

Do not   →   Don't
It is   →   It's
They are   →   They're

You try: Would not → _____

Sometimes, more than one letter is taken out:

Cannot   →   Can't
Shall not   →   Shan't (not sha'n't)
Could have →   Could've

You try: Should have → _____

2 To show that something belongs to, or is somehow connected with, something else:

When the word is singular, add **'s** :

The dog has a tail   The dog**'s** tail
The Prime Minister has an office   The Prime Minister**'s** office
Trudy has a terrapin   Trudy**'s** terrapin
Dad has a migraine   Dad**'s** migraine

You try: David has a mountain bike → _____

When the word is plural, add **'** without an 's':

The horses have a stable   The horses**'** stable
The players have a meeting   The players**'** meeting
The judges make a decision   The judges**'** decision
Two weeks is the length of the holiday   Two weeks**'** holiday

You try: The swans have a nest → _____

Apostrophes

Exceptions

1 If a word is plural, but does not end in 's', add **'s** :

> The children have toys   The children**'s** toys
> The women are kind   The women**'s** kindness

2 Singular words which end with an '*iz*' sound and have more than one vowel sound (syllable) usually take **'** only:

> **So:** Moses   Moses**'** family   **But:** Liz   Liz**'s** book
>   Jeff Bridges   Jeff Bridges**'** new film

3 The following possessive pronouns do not have apostrophes:

> **his**   **hers**   **ours**   **yours**   **theirs**

4 **its** means 'of it', as in 'The dog wagged **its** tail.'

5 **it's** means 'it is', as in '**It's** a lovely day today.'

What goes wrong?

The biggest mistake students make is to use apostrophes in plural words where they are not needed. What is wrong with the sentences below?

> I will have baked bean's and potatoe's.
> We have load's of video's.
> Volvo's are very safe cars.

The apostrophes are not needed as there are no missing letters, and the words are not showing that they possess anything.

There is also no need to put apostrophes after figures and abbreviations:

> 1890s, 1990s   not   1890's, 1990's
> MPs, MBEs   not   MP's, MBE's

Golden rules for apostrophes

- If in doubt, check.
- If you can't, *leave it out* (and check later).
- Above all, do not put apostrophes in words because they have an 's' at the end.

87

Apostrophes

Activity

Imagine you have a younger brother who has been asked by his teacher to correct a story he has written entitled 'The first time I ate worms'. The teacher has read the story and told him that he has got his apostrophes in a muddle. The corrections are his homework task, and he is allowed to get help. Knowing that you love this sort of thing (grammar, not worms) so much, he has asked you to assist. Re-write his story using apostrophes correctly.

The first time I ate worm's

Once upon a time, when I was three year's old, I was playing at the bottom of the garden with my sister Sally. We'd been making mud pie's and spotting ourselve's with mud so that it would look like we'd got the measle's. Sally had scooped up some slithery, blobby frog spawn out of Dad's pond. She was mixing it with weeds, rose petal's and Dads shaving cream to make a medicine.

'Do'nt worry,' she said, 'its going to cure us of the deadly lurgy.'

I didnt fancy it myself. Id had spaghetti for the first time the evening before, and was mad about it: I wanted to feel those lovely squidgy string's slipping down my throat again.

Then I caught sight of a worm's tail end sliding away into the earth, so I made a grab and pulled on it, stretching it until it's body nearly snapped in half. It came up with a plop, and there it was, all damp and slippery in my finger's. Without a moment's hesitation, I popped the slithering coil's into my mouth…

Colons and Semi-colons

Colons

You can use a colon to introduce a list of items:

> Here are the things that you will need for this experiment: a penknife, two paper clips, a piece of string and an African elephant.

You can also use a colon between two clauses when the second one explains or gives more information about the first:

> Cyanide gas is highly dangerous: anyone inhaling it can be killed in seconds.

A colon can also be used to introduce a saying or rule:

> Remember the golden rule of mountain life: don't eat yellow snow.

Semi-colons

Semi-colons are used to break up long sentences and lists:

> *The new Lada Hedgehog GTi has all the refinements you would expect: a 240-valve, V60 supercharged engine which runs on unleaded Heineken; electrically operated seats which recline automatically in traffic jams; a minibar; a complete sound system with automatic tuning.*

> *Each was silent, contemplating the next move: Danielle sat motionless on the sofa, staring blankly ahead of her; Belinda stood near the door, lazily turning over the pages of Good Homemaking; Geoff gazed out of the window at nothing, sighing in dissatisfaction.*

Semi-colons are also used to join clauses which are closely related:

> *The impossible we do at once; miracles take a little longer.*

Activity

Write out the following paragraph, putting in the colons and semi-colons where they should go.

> *Katie was looking forward to the holiday. She had packed everything walking boots, thick socks, waterproof and the map. She thought back to when they had discussed the route - Ben working it out carefully Tracy saying we shouldn't plan it Sarah and Michael thinking only about where we would eat. She wondered whether to pack an extra jumper as the wind along the coast could be freezing - as someone had said last time better safe than sorry!*

Speech marks

If you want to write down the words that someone actually speaks, or quote someone else's written words, you need to use **speech marks**.

In the cartoon, we can see what the characters are saying from the speech bubbles. In order to write down the conversation without pictures, we replace the bubbles with speech marks: ' '.

> 'What are you doing?' Dave asked.
>
> 'I'm trying to download the software for *Decimator*. It's a new virtual reality war game,' Pam replied.

You write the third speech: John said   _____

Rules for using speech marks

1 When a character first starts to speak:
- start a new paragraph
- indent the first line
- open speech marks '
- begin with a capital letter.

2 When a character stops speaking:
- end with a full stop, comma, question mark or exclamation mark, as needed
- then close the speech marks '.

Speech marks

To open new speech
1 start a new line
2 indent the line
3 open speech marks
4 use a capital letter

To close speech
1 full stop, comma, question mark or exclamation mark which goes inside speech marks in full sentences
2 close speech marks

> *I had to stop writing because Father just came in. He hardly ever comes in my room, so I knew at once something was wrong.*
>
> *'You all right?' he said, standing in the doorway. 'What've you been up to?'*
>
> *'Nothing,' I said. 'Why?'*
>
> *'Old man Jenkins. He said he saw you down on Rushy Bay.'*
>
> *'I was just collecting the wood,'* <u>*I told him as calmly as I could,*</u> *'like you said I should.' I find lying so difficult. I'm just not good at it.*

Interrupted speech
1 comma where speech breaks off
2 close speech marks
3 words not spoken by character
4 comma
5 re-open speech marks
6 no capital letter for re-opened speech
7 close speech as usual

> *Anna said that when she lied she had a particular 'look in her eye', which always gave her away.*

Punctuation outside speech marks where only a few words quoted

Mistakes to avoid

1 Forgetting to start new lines:

'I've found it!' 'Where was it?' 'Under the cushion.'

If your speech marks are touching, you have made a mistake

2 Putting speech marks round the ordinary text instead of the words people speak:

She's very late 'he said' I can't imagine where she's got to.

3 Putting the closing punctuation after the speech marks instead of before:

'These speech marks are driving me crazy'!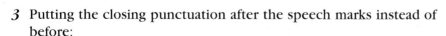

Activity

Write a short conversation between two people. One of them has a secret and the other is trying to find out what it is. Swap your story with a partner, and underline any mistakes in speech marks.

Unit 8: Common errors

This unit looks at mistakes which commonly occur in students' writing. You should use this for reference. If your teacher picks up mistakes in your writing that are covered here, use these activities for practice so that you get it right next time.

Would/Should/Could have

Students sometimes use the word '*of*' where they should use the word '*have*'. This may be because the shortened version of 'have' sounds like 'of':

> They could have walked twenty miles. → They could've walked twenty miles.

Because the letters *ve* after the apostrophe sound like *of*, some people make the mistake of writing:

> They could **of** walked twenty miles.

This is like writing 'I of done it' instead of 'I have done it', or 'They of two cars' instead of 'They have two cars'.

Activity 1

Write out and correct the sentences below. Write out in full the words with apostrophes, and make sure that '*have*' and '*of*' are always used correctly.

1 He will be here in the next five minutes, I should've thought.

2 I might of known that you would let me down, although I would've hoped you would stick by me.

3 Why did you shout at her? She would've agreed to discuss it if you had kept quiet. You shouldn't of created a scene.

4 I could've danced all night, but I would of missed my exam the next morning.

5 They've told us before that there could of been more people if you had put up more of your posters.

6 It couldn't of been Ray: if he had done it, he would've been late for school.

7 I would love to of seen Rebekah – she should've come for tea.

8 Why would they've said that? They should of kept it a secret.

Your/You're, Who's/Whose

Your and *you're* are often used incorrectly because they sound the same.

Your

Your means 'something belonging to you':

That's **your** pen; this is mine.   Can I borrow **your** ruler?

You're

You're is the shortened form of *you are*:

You are joking, aren't you?   →   **You're** joking, aren't you?

Activity 2

Here are some sentences with *your* and *you're* muddled up. Not all the uses are wrong, though, so you need to decide which ones are incorrect and write them out correctly.

1 Your standing in the wrong queue, you know. What's your name?

2 Well, your entitled to your opinion, but I think your absolutely wrong.

3 I wish I had seen you're new trainers. Your really lucky to have them.

Whose and *who's* have exactly the same sound, but their uses are very different.

Whose

Whose is used for people and things. It links the different parts of a sentence and shows how the words around it are connected to each other:

This is Dave, **whose** <u>sister</u> you met at the club.

Whose is also used in questions to ask 'belonging to whom?'

Whose pen is that?

Who's

Who's is the shortened form of '**who is**':

Who is going to tell him?   →   **Who's** going to tell him?

Activity 3

Choose whether it is correct to put *whose* or *who's* in the blanks and write out the sentences correctly. Try *who is* in the blank first. If it fits the sense of the sentence, *who's* is right. If it doesn't, put *whose*.

1 I don't know _____ bag it is.

2 I bet it's Dave _____ behind all of this.

3 I'm not sure _____ list you've got. _____ on it?

93

There/Their/They're

There, **their** and **they're** are often used incorrectly as they sound the same. When you are writing or checking your work, you must look hard at every example of these words and ask yourself, 'Have I used the right spelling?'

Here's what each one means:

There

There means 'in that place':

> The sports centre is over **there**.   **There**'s the ball.
> Your brother is still **there**.   She went **there** with her friend.

There is also used as part of a statement:

> **There** is a wasp in the classroom.

Their

Their means 'belonging to or connected with them':

> That's **their** train. ──────────→ (the train **they** want to take)
> **Their** house is bigger than ours.   (the house **they** live in)

They're

They're is a shortened form of 'they are':

> **They are** bound to win.   →   **They're** bound to win.
> If **they are** going, I'll go too.   →   If **they're** going, I'll go too.

Activity 4

Look carefully at each blank in these sentences and decide whether the right word for the blank is **there**, **their** or **they're**. Write out the complete sentences correctly.

1 I want you to be _____ when they arrive with _____ friends.

2 _____ the biggest-selling band this year, and _____ new album, *Rats On Toast*, is already at Number One.

3 _____ bags are over _____ by the door, and _____ getting in people's way.

4 We don't know _____ names, but _____ are fifteen in the group.

5 _____ won't be time for them to visit _____ friends: _____ tied up all week with the project.

Two/Too/To

Two, *too* and *to* have the same sound, so they can easily be confused:

Two

Two is the number 2, as in 'two cats and two mice'.

Too

Too means 'an excessively large or small amount of something':

You've given me **too** much sauce.	(A *larger* amount than I wanted)
Too few people turned up to make it worthwhile.	(A *smaller* number than we wanted)

Too also means 'as well':

Polly is coming **too**.	Have you seen it, **too**?

To

To is used in all cases where *two* and *too* do not apply. You can often recognise it because, when you say it, it sounds 'shorter' than *two* or *too*:

I would like **to** go **to** the pictures.

Activity 5

Look carefully at each blank in these sentences. Write out the sentences with the correct word from *two*, *too* or *to* in the blanks:

1 I went clubbing with _____ of my mates last night, but we were _____ tired _____ stay up all night.

2 We are pleased _____ receive the money, but it's a case of _____ little _____ late.

3 If you're coming _____ , you'll need _____ get hold of _____ sets.

4 Mandy wasn't _____ impressed when she discovered what Gary had done _____ her bike.

5 _____ many adults fail _____ appreciate the pressures on children _____ succeed.

6 She was in _____ much of a hurry _____ notice that Peter was getting on the bus _____ .

Where/Were/We're

Where, *were* and *we're* do not all sound the same when spoken, but they are still easy to muddle up. Here is the correct way to use them:

Where

Where is used in questions, and means 'in which place?':

> **Where** are you?   **Where** did you put my books?

Where also links the different parts of a sentence and shows how the words around it are connected with each other:

> This is the <u>spot</u> **where** <u>the accident happened</u>.

Were

Were is part of the verb *be*:

Present	Past
I **am**	I **was**
You **are**	You **were**

> You **were** going into the shop when I saw you.
> What **were** you going to buy?

We're

We're is the shortened form of '*we are*':

> **We are** just good friends.   →   **We're** just good friends.
> **We are** going to win this time.   →   **We're** going to win this time.

Activity 6

Look carefully at each blank in these sentences. Write out the sentences with the correct word from *where*, *were* or *we're* in the blanks:

1 _____ going to visit Aunty Jean on Sunday.

2 _____ _____ you when I called last night?

3 The Hammerheads _____ going to meet at the spot _____ Bob was attacked.

4 I don't know _____ _____ going to put all these toys that _____ in the loft.

5 _____ you not in school on the day when we _____ told _____ to stand for the presentations?

6 If I _____ you, I would avoid any places _____ there's likely to be trouble.